Free at Last

How to Be Set Free Through Forgiveness

Gloria Lundstrom

LOWELL LUNDSTROM Ministries
Sisseton, South Dakota 57262
Box 4000, Winnipeg, Manitoba R3C 3W1

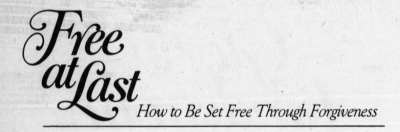

Free at Last

How to Be Set Free Through Forgiveness

Copyright © 1983
Gloria Lundstrom
Sisseton, South Dakota 57262

ISBN 0-938220-52-7

Printed in the United States of America.

All biblical quotations are taken from the King James Version unless otherwise noted.

Credits

I want to give special thanks to Bruce Schoeman and Sally Petersen for the guidance and encouragement they gave me in writing my first book. Special thanks also to my typists Gloria Hutchins, Lynn Groves and Charlene Van Riper for efforts beyond the call of duty. I'm convinced God gave me the right people to work with to bring this book about.

Dedication

With loving appreciation I dedicate this book to my husband and sweetheart of 18 years, Larry; to our two lovely daughters, LaShawn and LaDawn; and to our little tiger, Lee Donovan. These four special people help make my life fulfilling and exciting.

Table of Contents

About the Author

Besides being a wife and mother of three children—two daughters and one son—Gloria Lundstrom is a gifted speaker and singer. She has ministered in city-wide crusades, family life seminars and women's outreaches while traveling with the Lowell Lundstrom Ministries throughout the United States and Canada for 18 years.

God has given her the desire and ability to touch peoples' hearts—enabling them to release destructive emotions collected over the years. This release through forgiveness has resulted in thousands of people being liberated from the emotions and feelings that bind and choke relationships with family, friends and God.

Gloria shares from her own past and from testimonies of those who have worked their way through tragic and hurtful memories to reach the peace and excitement of liberated living. You will be able to experience this personal freedom by reading and responding to this book of ministry.

Gloria welcomes opportunities to minister for Christ. You may contact her by writing to the following address:

Larry Lundstrom Family Ministry
P.O. Box 99
Sisseton, South Dakota 57262
Or call:
(605) 698-3939 or 698-3900

Introduction

In this book I will share some fantastic victories that have taken place in hundreds of lives. I'm also excited about what Christ has done for me. I'm not the same person I used to be, and I know by the time you finish reading this book, you won't be the same person either. God will show you areas in your life that will help you on the road to personal freedom. Let me pray with you right now.

Dear Heavenly Father, right now I pray that You will place Your loving arms around this precious person reading this book, and that by Your Holy Spirit You will begin to reveal and release anything in their life that has been keeping them from Your blessings. Lord, make them willing to be totally open to Your Spirit and to Your leading. I ask this in the precious name of Jesus, Amen.

Prologue

The alarm clock in my son's room kept ringing. The night seemed too short. My body refused to wake up so I pulled the covers up again and buried my head deeper into my fluffy feather pillow. The alarm continued to clatter. I thought, "Why isn't my son turning it off? Why isn't he getting up?" Annoyed, I pulled myself out of bed, slipped on my housecoat, marched down the hallway and rapped on Brian's door. He didn't answer. By this time his younger sister had awakened and joined me by the bedroom door. I began to feel uneasy. Cautiously I opened the door. My eyes fell on Brian's body, half off the bed, lying in a pool of blood with a gun lying nearby. Fear gripped me as I ran in and frantically grabbed his wrist...there was no pulse. I wanted to shake him and scream, "Hey, Brian, this is no time for a joke. This has gone far enough, now, get up!" But it wasn't a joke. He wasn't responding—it was evident that he was DEAD! He had shot himself. "But why?" I screamed inside, "Why did you do this, Brian? Why would you kill yourself just at the prime of your life?" He was only 20 years old. My mind began spinning, my body became weak. Horror gripped me.

Only a few hours earlier I had looked in Brian's room to see if he was home yet. The room was empty. I had felt a growing concern for him the past few weeks because he was depressed and wouldn't say why. But the last few days his spirits seemed high again and I was encouraged. When I noticed he wasn't home yet at one o'clock a.m., I prayed to God that He would bring him home safely. Only hours earlier Brian was full of life, a big, strong, healthy boy. He always had a joke or a grin. Now the house felt like a tomb. There was no joking, laughing, chiding—only the silence of death hovering over the house. Numbly I called my husband who was away working in Minneapolis. Then the ambulance came and took Brian's body away.

The feelings that seized me the following days were overwhelming. The unbelievable had happened. I felt both grief and guilt. Was it my fault? Could I have avoided this tragedy? I became bitter and angry toward God. Where was He? Why did He allow this to happen? Then I became bitter and disgusted toward Brian. How could he be so selfish as to take his own life, robbing me of the joy he had brought me? He was the sunshine of my life. Not only was he my son, but he was my buddy. He helped me take care of the house because my husband was gone so much. I cherished the moments around dinner time when I was preparing food. He'd bounce in and suggest, "Mom, I'd better taste it to see if it's O.K." Then he'd snitch a bite and laugh. I loved every moment. But now he is gone. Gone forever. My heart aches, "Oh, God, why? Why Brian? Why did you do this to me...why, why, why?"

This sounds like a fictitious story, but it isn't. It is the true story of the Miner family from La Crosse, Wisconsin, whose lives were ripped apart at the seams emotionally, physically and spiritually. They have spent many sleepless nights reliving this nightmare. The Miners are not the only family whose lives have been tragically altered. Every day thousands of homes and lives are being shattered by death, disease, divorce, hurt, fear, rejection. I'll never forget what Brian's mother told me the night she related her story. "Gloria, death and suffering are so uncertain. You never know whose door it's going to knock on next."

I'm 38 years old, and I've found that statement to

be absolutely true. It seems much of my life has been spent either entering a struggle or trying to get out of one. No one is exempt from suffering, pain or death. It is no respector of persons—it strikes the rich and the poor, the intellectual and the illiterate, the healthy and the sickly of all ages.

Now that we know no one is exempt from life's struggles, where do we go from here? How do we deal with hurts, death, divorce, sickness, fear, bitterness? How do we cope with these feelings that are bound up deep within us?

These questions and many others are answered in this book.

Hang on! You're on your way!

1

Lord, Set Me Free

I'm so frustrated. I feel imprisoned. Why do I feel this way? What's blocking God's blessing in my life?'' I can vividly recall the inner anguish gnawing, eating away at me as I sat in the back bedroom of our bus, blankly staring out the window as the Minnesota countryside rushed by. The sun was sinking below the horizon; summer had ended. The first cold days of fall had arrived, nipping the leaves and giving them their long-awaited chance to begin their parade of colors. It was beautiful, but somehow I failed to enjoy it.

Confusion raged within me. I curled up in the corner of the bed and sank my head into the pillow. Again questions crowded my mind. ''Why can't I sing freely? What's hindering me from being able to speak freely at meetings, seminars and crusades? Why haven't I been able to love and accept myself?'' In desperation I cried, ''Oh, God, I feel imprisoned! You just have to set me free!'' With those words still ringing in my ears, I fell asleep.

We traveled all night enroute to a Lundstrom Family Life Seminar in Kansas. I woke up feeling as if I hadn't slept at all. I packed, took the children into a motel and scurried to speak at the ladies' session. The Lord blessed the lives of those women who came seeking encouragement in their own lives and marriages. I was thankful for that, but I still had that deep frustration burning within me—I could actually feel it.

God is Listening

After counseling several ladies I began to leave the meeting room when I heard a small, timid voice. "Gloria, could I please speak with you for a moment?" There she stood, only about 4 feet 10 inches, a petite, modestly dressed brunette. She looked up at me, then dropped her eyes and chin in embarrassment as she stammered, "Umm...mmm...Gloria, yesterday as I was getting packed to come to this seminar, the Lord spoke to my heart and told me I should bring this book and give it to you." Then she blushed again. "Um," she continued, "this has never happened before, but I'm just trying to be obedient to God, so here!" She shoved the book into my hand and quickly disappeared. At that moment someone else walked up to be counseled. I sandwiched the book between my Bible and seminar materials until I finished talking.

A few minutes later, on the way to another session, I remembered the book and thought, "I wonder what this book is about and why the Lord told that lady to give it to me?" I picked it up. To my complete astonishment the title *Set Free* jumped off the cover—the very words that had been my heart's cry for weeks! My heart leaped. I knew this was from God. I was overwhelmed to think that God loved me *so* much that He would speak to the heart of a meek little lady in Kansas I had never met before and tell her to bring me the book I needed.

I walked over to a quiet corner in the long corridor and prayed, "Oh Jesus, thank you for hearing my prayer." I didn't know what the book was about—but I had a feeling something good was about to happen in my life.

2

What Is Inner Healing?

*T*he rest of that day was so busy I didn't get a chance to look at my new book. I came back to the room at midnight fatigued. I fell into bed, oblivious to everything. Suddenly the words "Set Free" popped into my mind. I jumped up, quickly grabbed the book, propped the pillows on the bed and began reading the cover again. There was a subtitle I hadn't noticed before. It read, *Set Free Through Inner Healing,* by Betty Tapscott. I had never heard of her before—and what was inner healing? I'd heard the term used, but really didn't know much about it.

God Heals Spiritually

I believed in spiritual healing because I experienced it back in April, 1952. I was a slim, shy little blonde Norwegian, 8 years old, chosen by God to be born into a family of 10 brothers—five older, five younger. (There were times I wondered if it was God who put me there—I fought brothers from all sides!) Through the years they'd tell me jokingly, "You're the thorn among us beautiful roses."

A few months ago my mother said, "Missy, you often wondered why God allowed you to be born in a family with 10 brothers. As a child you used to say, 'Mom, I know I got here by mistake. What actually happened was that the baskets at the hospital got mixed up and I ended up with the wrong mother and went to the wrong home. I can't believe that a God of love would ever allow me to have to put up with 10 brothers!'" Mom continued, "But do you know what? I think God knew if you could grow up, live and survive 10 brothers, Gloria, you could survive anything—He was preparing you for the ministry and living on the road!"

On a spring Sunday evening in April, 1952, my family was invited to visit the Assembly of God church in Sisseton, South Dakota. We had heard that they did a lot of singing there and we loved music, so we all packed into the old station wagon—feet and legs hanging out everywhere.

That night the minister spoke from the Word of God. I don't remember the sermon text or the Scripture he used, but I do remember feeling something inside of me. The minister invited those who wanted to ask Jesus Christ into their hearts to come forward to the altar. He said by asking God to forgive our sins and receiving Jesus into our hearts we can know that when we die we can go to heaven for eternity. (I knew that word meant forever and forever.) That sounded wonderful! I'd heard of this place called hell and about the eternal fire where you would burn and burn forever. I knew for sure I didn't want to go there!

When the preacher urged, "Come!" our whole family stood up and walked forward. Even as I walked up the aisle, I felt as if heavy blankets were falling off

15

my shoulders. The minute I knelt at the altar and prayed, "Jesus, I love you!", it seemed all heaven opened and His joy, peace and happiness came into my heart. I was so happy I started to giggle. I felt free. It was beautiful! Then, just as if someone was kneeling beside me whispering in my ear, I heard a voice softly say, "Gloria, I want you to be a minister's or an evangelist's wife." I looked around. Nobody was there. Then I knew God was speaking to my heart. He called me to serve Him full-time. That very moment I felt like a new girl. I felt so clean, free and happy. That is why I believe in spiritual healing. It happened to me.

God Heals Physically

I also believe in physical healing. God has healed me many times through the years. While growing up I was known as the "sick chick." Everything that came along I got. I was like a human vacuum: I'd pick up every germ and would end up seriously sick either at home in bed or in the local hospital. It got to be a joke among the nurses there. One day they quipped, "Why don't you just buy a room here?" When I'd leave they would say, "Well, when will you be back? We'll keep a room open for you." But, praise God, He always intervened and brought me through.

Eight years ago I became seriously ill and for weeks I couldn't keep food down. I was going into comas; extremely low blood sugar and total exhaustion took a toll on the organs of my body—almost to the point of death. After a series of medical tests were taken, the doctors called my husband and said, "The tests have shown there is almost no medical reason why your wife is even alive. Rush her to the hospital. You may as well plan her funeral."

Stunned and shocked, Larry, Lowell and the team went before the throne of God in prayer. They rallied groups of friends and partners all over the U.S. to pray for me. God responded. He delights to step in when medical doctors say "no hope." God gives *living hope*. God honored the prayers of all His people and began to heal me.

The doctor had said, "If she comes out of this, she will be confined to bed for another six to nine months." But because of a miracle-working God, I went home in less than four weeks. I've encountered many near-death experiences in my life, but God had other plans for me. He had a purpose for my life. He allowed me to be healed. I am living proof of God's physical healing.

Test Your Memory

Back to the book—I sat up reading most of the night. The words "inner healing" had me puzzled. They even sounded mysterious. But I didn't care how puzzling or mysterious inner healing was—I wanted to know more about it. I began reading again. Betty Tapscott talked about how our lives are affected by our past. You see, our conscious mind is basically very kind to us—things, incidents, words, events can happen to us that we forget quickly—but our subconscious mind is a diary of our entire life. Just like an all-purpose computer, it records every smell, every sight, every sound, everything we've touched and everything we've tasted. Any time the subconscious decides it wants to, it can flip any memory out of its memory bank and shoot it up to the conscious. Immediately we can relive bits and pieces of our life. Here's a test—try it!

I want you to let your subconscious take over for a minute or two. I want you to reach in your memory bank. Go back to your childhood—between six and ten years old. Can you recall a special Christmas during those years? Picture where your Christmas tree stood; see the Christmas gifts under it. Visualize picking up a gift and shaking and touching it, guessing what it is. Can you smell that delicious aroma of Christmas— fresh, hot cookies and cakes that your mother or grand-mother carefully removed from the oven? Maybe you can even hear your mother say, "You can have *just one* cookie—we are going to save the rest for Christmas!" Can you recall the joy and excitement when Christmas Eve finally arrives, yuletide carols being sung, relatives gathering together, the shrills of children's laughter? Excitement fills the air as you open your gifts.

Right now, everyone reading this is experiencing memories from the subconscious memory bank. These memories now trigger different feelings. For most of you, you feel joy and happiness. Your conscious now says, "That's good, I like it, it's been fun—I'd like to relive it."

Now let's try another experiment. Open your memory bank again and go back to a time when you were very sick—high temperature, pain, discomfort. Many of you may have ended up in the hospital. Right now your memory is releasing that scene: you can see the bed where you lay, you can remember words spoken to you by concerned family or friends. You can recall tender loving care from your mom or dad. You can almost feel the tenderness of someone's hand rubbing yours or your forehead to help ease your pain and to comfort you. This incident brings about different feelings. You are experiencing a flash-back of pain, discomfort, fear. All these feelings register, "I want to block this memory out of my mind. I don't want to relive it. Send it back to the memory bank!''

Here's a third experiment. Let your memory bank now take you back to a time where someone falsely accused, cheated or physically hurt you. Remember when someone deserted or divorced you, put you in a foster home or made fun of you. Think of one or two incidents that have happened to you in the past year, month, week or day. Now what feelings are being released—disgust, hatred, hurt, bitterness, rejection, feelings of being unwanted or unloved?

Your Past Is Always Present

In the last few paragraphs you have relived not only memories, but also the feelings that accompany them. Now, whether you want to admit it or not—all these feelings have left an enormous impact upon your life. They have affected your self-worth, self-acceptance, your relationship with your husband or wife, children, parents, employer/employees, church and job. Your feelings also influence activities you participate in and goals that you have. They affect your whole life.

Not only do these feelings and memories affect us— but tragically we can become imprisoned by them. These feelings can keep us from becoming the person we wish to become; they discourage us from daring to believe in ourselves, or to step out in faith, or to take a risk. If we realize where this all starts, then we can go back and begin to remedy it.

What we are today is a result of our past. The devil will try to rule us by our past. *Did you know that the devil will bring up our past to keep us from God's future?* Does the devil ever come to you and bring up your past and try to discourage you? He has done it to me. But let me tell you something. Whenever Satan comes and brings up your past, if you can mentally visualize him, point a finger at him and say, "Listen, Old Slewfoot, your past isn't so good either." Then, go one step further. Confront him and say, "I'll tell you something more—your future is pretty dark!" Satan has no future. You have a future in Jesus Christ and Satan does not. He cannot have any control over your life if you let Christ control you. This is why inner healing is so important. Many Christians are physically well, but are emotionally and spiritually crippled. Jesus wants us to be completely whole and free.

What Is Inner Healing?

Inner healing is the healing of the inner man; the soul of man is his mind, will and emotions. It is the process that through prayer we are set free from fear, self-pity, guilt, feelings of resentment, rejection and condemnation that keep us in bondage to self and to Satan.

Three healings you can experience:

1. SPIRITUAL HEALING—being saved from your sins.

2. PHYSICAL HEALING—God healing you from sickness and disease.

3. INNER HEALING—peace that Christ puts within your mind, will and emotions (the emphasis of this book).

All in all, Christ wants us to be completely whole. Isaiah 53:5 tells us what Jesus did for us, *"He was wounded and bruised for our sins. He was chastised that we might have peace, he was lashed—and we were healed"* (TLB).

Scriptures On Inner Healing

Here are some verses that I know will help you as you go through the process of inner healing. Tear these verses out and put them where you will see them and think about them every day—on your bedroom mirror, your refrigerator door, etc. I know you will be blessed and strengthened by these powerful words.

2 Corinthians 3:17 (KJV)—*"...where the Spirit of the Lord is, there is liberty."*

2 Timothy 1:7 (KJV)—*"For God hath not given us the spirit of fear; but of power, and of love, and of a sound mind."*

Philippians 3:13 (TLB)—*"...Forgetting the past and looking forward to what lies ahead...."*

Isaiah 9:4 (TLB)—*"For God will break the chains that bind his people and the whip that scourges them...."*

Hebrews 13:8 (RSV)—*"Jesus Christ is the same yesterday, today and for ever."*

Jeremiah 6:14 (TLB)—*"You can't heal a wound by saying it's not there!"*

Matthew 18:18 (TLB)—*"...whatever you bind on earth is bound in heaven, and whatever you free on earth will be freed in heaven."*

Psalm 51:10 (TLB)—*"Create in me a new, clean heart, O God, filled with clean thoughts and right desires."*

Psalm 147:3 (TLB)—*"He heals the brokenhearted, binding up their wounds."*

Isaiah 26:3 (TLB)—*"He will keep in perfect peace all those who trust in him, whose thoughts turn often to the Lord!"*

Luke 4:18-19 (TLB)—*"The Spirit of the Lord is upon me...he has sent me to announce that captives shall be released and the blind shall see, that the downtrodden shall be freed from their oppressors...."*

John 14:27 (TLB)—*"I am leaving you with a gift—peace of mind and heart!"*

Romans 12:2 (KJV)—*"...be not conformed to this world: but be ye transformed by the renewing of your mind...."*

Philippians 4:7 (TLB)—*"...His peace will keep your thoughts and your hearts quiet and at rest as you trust in Christ Jesus."*

3

The Foundation

*F*our years ago the Lord gave us the opportunity to move from our "little brown house," as we called it, to a larger home in Sisseton, South Dakota. We loved the little house—it had many precious memories —but when our son, Lee Donovan, was born we suddenly outgrew it. Besides that, the basement had a ceiling that was six feet high and my husband, Larry, measures six feet, three inches. You guessed it—every time he'd go downstairs where we had all of our musical instruments I'd hear the death howl, "Oh, no, it hurts!" I'd race down and there he'd stand with that silly, sheepish grin on his face, holding his right hand over the bloody indentation newly acquired on his forehead and he'd admit, "Yeah, I forgot again." Then he'd add, "I hate this low ceiling...."

When the Lord brought us to a larger home with a higher ceiling the first thing Larry said was, "Oh, great! I won't have to bang my head anymore!"

A House Divided

After moving to our new home, we thought all of our problems were over and we would live happily ever after. Well—that's not quite the way it happened. After a few days, we noticed a large crack in the driveway. Three or four months later, the brickwork around the flower box and entryway began to crack, followed by settling in the foyer. Then the closet doors began dropping off and the doors shifted in the three bedrooms so they wouldn't close. Later we saw a big crack running across the entire family room floor. Last July, we stopped in Sisseton for a few hours on our way to Colorado and noticed a wide crack right down the center of our living and dining rooms. This house had looked so perfect, so flawless. It was only one year old when we bought it. Now after three years it was a mess! We were sick. We called in contractors to find the cause of the problem. They brought in their heavy equipment and shovels and began digging. I stood nearby holding my breath—wondering what the outcome would be. To our shock, water began pouring out from under the foundation, verifying a break in the water pipe.

The two men lay their shovels down, looked up at Larry with dismay and reported, "We've been building houses for over 30 years and we have never seen a house settle and fall apart like this one. You'll have to go back and start all over at the foundation. First, jack up the house, repair the water pipe break, stabilize the foundation, repair the damage caused by settling, pour new concrete for the driveway, sidewalks, family room floor, and re-landscape. If you don't follow through with these procedures, the house will continue to settle and crack."

"Larry and Gloria, it's going to cost you thousands of dollars plus the heartache of tearing it apart. It would be much easier to build another home. Really, the whole thing is going to be a nightmare."

The other contractor looked at me and commented, "Gloria, when you drive by from a distance, the house looks great! You have it decorated so cute and cozy. But when you take your eyes off of the knick-knacks and furnishings, it makes you sick to see the damage. It looks great at a distance—but it's a disaster up close!"

My heart sank. I sat back on the grass and thought, "Wow, what an illustration!" What if someone was able to dig into the depths of my life, under my foundation? What would they find? Would they find me clean, secure and stable with Christ-centered footings? Oh, I know they'd find Christ on the surface—but what would they find when they got below the subconscious level of my mind? Would my foundation be solid or would it be shot through with cracks of anger, bitterness, hatred, guilt, impure thoughts, dissentions, deceit? Only the Lord knew how desperately I wanted to be clean and transparent so only Christ would be seen in my life.

Christ: The Solid Rock

This restoration (or cleaning) comes only by inner healing. In the second chapter of Corinthians, Paul tells us the way to experience complete inner healing, *"Casting down imaginations, and every high thing that exalteth itself against the knowledge of God, and bringing into captivity every thought to the obedience of Christ"* (2 Corinthians 10:5, KJV).

Our actions and reactions lurk beneath the surface of our lives waiting for a chance to pop through. Our job is not to run busily over the surface of our "lake" making sure no "waves" appear, but to let Christ bring them to surface; to see ourselves as we really are, confess our sins, thank God for the cleansing and ask Him to change our hearts and lives.

At first I thought that task would be impossible—so many things began to bob up on the surface of my lake. By faith, I had to let the Holy Spirit work on one problem at a time. He helped me to pull down unhealthy imaginations. He enabled me to dredge up other unresolved conflicts from my memory so I could deal with them and release them to God. The Lord assured me of His forgiveness for the sins and guilts of my past. Only then could I become transparent. What a liberating, freeing feeling—the more I cleaned out, the more of Christ I let fill that vacant spot. I began to sense Him alive, deep within—not just on the surface of my life.

Now I knew it was really possible to become what Christ wanted me to be. Friend, it's possible for you, too. Paul commanded in Romans 12:2 for my mind to be actually transformed. Romans 8:29 states, *"I was predestined to be conformed to the image of His Son."*

Galatians 5:16 admonishes, *"Walk in the Spirit, and ye shall not fulfill the lust of the flesh."* Then, in Ephesians 3:16 and 17 a promise was made to the Ephesians, *"That he would grant you, according to the riches of his glory, to be strengthened with might by His Spirit in the inner man; that Christ may dwell in your hearts by faith."* Again, He said, *"...put off concerning the former conversation the old man, which is corrupt according to the deceitful lusts; and be renewed in the spirit of your mind; And that ye put on the new man, which after God is created in righteousness and true holiness"* (Ephesians 4:22-24).

28

What I desired and what you desire is not an impossibility! It is to be the goal of every believer of Jesus Christ. Being conformed to His image does not begin with an outward expression, but with the healing of the inner man (subconscious). In other words, the best way to clean up the surface of our lake is not by skimming the top—but by purifying the source of water from the well-springs at the bottom. As Christians, we must be committed to a walk of absolute obedience to Christ in our conscious life. We must carefully guard the gates of our ears and eyes and especially that of our mouths. We need to stand guard at the doorpost of our mind to repel each evil thought by which Satan would gain entry.

Ask the Lord to help you hunt out those thoughts, deeds, sins and guilts that have bound you, so they can be confessed, forgiven and forgotten—in the name of Jesus.

If the Holy Spirit is to have completely free access to minister to all areas of our subconscious, He must be invited in. We must dare to be open to whatever surfaces, knowing that through faith in Jesus Christ victory will be ours.

Let's pray together and ask God to open your heart to inner healing in your life:

Lord, I ask You to take complete control of my inner man. Lord, I open myself to You. Protect me and don't allow the enemy to have any part of this time together. I ask You to go to the corners of my conscious and subconscious mind and bring to surface, to my memory, the sins and guilts of the past that are destroying my spiritual foundation. I ask You to make me willing to release all the sins so You can begin inner healing in my life. In Jesus' name, Amen.

4

The Rose

At the time I was praying for God to "set me free," I was busy traveling, singing, recording, and speaking at seminars and luncheons. I loved the Lord. I felt His hand upon my life, but there was something hindering the total joy I was longing to feel. I repeated John 10:10 over and over—*"The thief cometh not, but for to steal, and to kill, and to destroy: I am come that they might have life, and that they might have it more abundantly."* I so desperately wanted to have that abundant life—to me that meant "freedom" and I didn't have it. I felt as if there was a big padlock on the container of God's blessing for my life and I couldn't find the key to it.

In my desperation to find God's release, I set aside a week to pray. I stormed heaven, but the more I read and prayed, the thicker the wall seemed to be. I just couldn't break through. I began to panic. "Oh, God, what is wrong?" Then the words of Betty Tapscott's book hit me.

Maybe you're missing the blessing of God on your life because of some deep, buried feelings of hatred, fear, bitterness and anger that are controlling you. Maybe you have haunting memories and scars from childhood that are basking in the subconscious, running the control panel of your life, and it's keeping you in bondage.

She went on,

You need to pray and ask God to bring to surface out of the subconscious all the feelings and memories that are blocking your life. You may have no idea what is buried there—ask God to bring it out, relive the incident and ask God for an inner healing—to take a spiritual eraser and remove the scars and memories that have imprisoned you. You can be set free to be a clean vessel for the Lord to begin a new work in and through you.

Journey Through Inner Healing

This revelation was a new concept to me as it may be to you. What followed was the beginning of a life-changing experience. Please walk with me on my journey through inner healing.

"I'm not giving up, Lord. If there is anything to this inner healing You'll have to show this stubborn Norwegian girl. If there is anything buried in my subconscious that shouldn't be there, release it so that I can be cleansed and become a new, clean vessel for Your use." I was tired of myself. I wanted to become a new creature in Christ. I was tired of being many faces—one personality when I was on stage; another with my family; another with relatives; another with the unsaved; another with my husband; another when I was speaking...I was sick of all those "Glorias." I didn't like any of them. I wanted to become a completely new creature in Christ. All these roles kept me in bondage

31

until I didn't know which one I really was. I felt like I was on the old TV program, "To Tell the Truth." Sometimes I'd scream inside, "Will the *real* Gloria Lundstrom PLEASE stand up!" I was scared to find out which one would step forward admitting the true identity.

As I was seeking God one night, the Lord spoke these words to my heart: "Gloria, do you really want to know why you are not free? Do you want Me to bless you and use you?" I cried out in excitement, "Oh yes, Lord, yes!"

"You are bitter against Me and I cannot bless you until you release that bitterness." That was it. Cut and dried.

I panicked, "Lord, don't leave me now!" I objected. "You know I'm not bitter against *You*—that's ridiculous! Why would I travel on the road 340 days out of the year in a stinky, cramped diesel bus if it wasn't for You? Half the time the air conditioning or heater doesn't work or the bus breaks down. I drag my three precious children all over the country like vagabonds, and we eat every meal in a cafe. Most of my clothes are ruined in scorching commercial dryers. I must do my showering in high school group shower rooms or truck stops. Lord, You've got to be kidding! I love You! I've given You my whole life! Why would You say that I am bitter?"

Just then I caught myself and thought, "Oh, oh, maybe there is something filed way down in my subconscious that I don't remember." Then the word "roses" flashed. It was as if I saw a neon sign in front of me. First on the left it would flash "bitterness" and then on the right the word "roses" would flash. Lord, what are You trying to tell me? Why do You keep reminding me of roses? You know I hate roses. Sure, I know, every woman is supposed to love a rose. It's a symbol of love—but not to me.

Larry used to bring me a rose about once a month right after we were married. He'd be proud as a peacock when he presented it to me. At first I would say, "Oh, Larry, thank you! I love it!" Then I'd smell it and WHAM, I hated the smell! I'd get nauseated, but even more than that I felt anger, disgust and bitterness mounting up instantly within me. Then I would shove it somewhere out of my smelling reach and hope it would die real fast. That rose always lived too long—even if I didn't add fresh water to it!

I pressed God, "Why are you reminding me of roses along with bitterness? If there is anything to this inner healing, Lord," I implored, "You show me why I'm bitter and why I hate roses." As soon as the words came out of my mouth, the Lord brought to my mind an incident that had happened to me when I was seven years old.

Roses Will Tell

It was May, 1951, on a Saturday afternoon. My Grandfather Brooks was visiting at our home that day. He was my best friend. I loved him so much and he loved me and I knew it—he showed it and I felt it. Almost every day we'd go for a stroll, hand in hand, and we'd talk and laugh and giggle. Grandpa was magic—it seemed he always found a penny or a nickel every time we went for a walk. He was a hero to me.

That particular Saturday afternoon Grandpa gave his special chuckle, knelt down and pulled me into his arms. With a dancing twinkle in his eye he announced, "Do you know what Grandpa is going to do for you on Monday?" I tingled with anticipation. He continued, "I'm going to build you a teeter-totter, just for you, on Monday." I was immediately airborne. I grabbed him around the neck and hugged and kissed him.

I declared, "Well, Grandpa, anything as important

as this means we have to draw out plans to make sure it will be the best one in town!'' (That was profound, because there was only one teeter-totter in Sisseton, a town of 3,000 people, and that was at the little city park!)

"Sure, honey, we'll make plans. Tomorrow after church you come to our apartment and we'll talk about it.''

Sunday noon came too slowly. As soon as church was dismissed I prodded everyone (my parents and eight brothers) into the car and Dad drove us to my grandparents' apartment. I jumped out of the car, ran up the old wooden stairway and threw open the white screen door. There stood Grandma—cleaning off the kitchen table. With a quick "Hello!" thrown in her direction I asked, "Where's Grandpa?''

She pointed, "He's in the bedroom.''

I ran in there only to find him sneaking a nap. Didn't he know this was no time for a nap? We had business to attend to. I tapped his shoulder, "Grandpa, wake up! We have to talk about my teeter-totter!''

He groggily opened his eyes, gave me that certain chuckle and pulled me close to him, "Hi, honey.''

I shouted, "Grandpa, you can't sleep now, we have to make plans for that teeter-totter right now!'' He tenderly tried to calm me down, reassuring me that all was O.K.

"Honey, Grandpa is tired and has a headache. I'll tell you what: why don't you go fishing with your dad and mom and then come back at 5 o'clock. I promise you we'll make plans for your teeter-totter then.'' I knew Grandpa always kept his promises, so I agreed.

We went fishing, but I made sure we were back at Grandpa's apartment at 5 o'clock sharp. I bounded up the stairway and tried to open the door. To my dismay it was locked. My father, following closely behind me, noticed a note taped to the window.

Nonchalantly he said, "We are going up to Uncle Ernie's and Aunt Helen's house."

I was relieved knowing where my grandparents were. We quickly reloaded into the car and went directly to my aunt and uncle's home. I leapt out of the car, ran inside, and saw my Grandma seated at the kitchen table. "Grandma, where's Grandpa?" I squealed.

"He's passed away," she said. Then she put her head in her hands and began crying.

"Well, which way did he go?" I quizzed. She didn't answer me and I didn't know what was wrong with her. I only wanted to find Grandpa. I ran to the dining room where other relatives were seated quietly around the table. Again I asked, "Where's my Grandpa?"

"He's gone," they said.

"Gone where?" I asked. I was tired of the run-around. I took my "poky" finger and jabbed my cousin's leg. "Tell me where my Grandpa is!" He just looked at me.

Then the thought hit me, "I'll bet that Grandpa is playing a trick on me. I'll bet he's upstairs taking another nap." I flew up the old staircase and searched all three bedrooms. The beds were neatly made. Something was wrong! Grandpa and Grandma were always together when all the relatives gathered. Where was he? I just saw him a couple of hours ago. My feet felt like they had lead weights attached to them as I began walking down the staircase.

I walked over to my cousin again. No more games. I demanded, "Where is my Grandpa?"

He gave me a little shove and said, "He's dead!"

The words, "He's dead!" rang in my ears. I wanted to deny them. "No, not my Grandpa! I love him! I need him—he's my best friend! He promised he would build my teeter-totter tomorrow, and he always keeps

35

his word. He loves me, he wouldn't leave me!'' I staggered over to a big, overstuffed chair, folded my legs under me, lay my head on the soft arm of the chair and tried to sort it all out in my mind. Nothing made sense. A little later my parents gathered all of us kids together and we went home. I went right to bed. I woke up hoping Grandpa's death was just a dream, but I knew it wasn't.

We went back to my uncle and aunt's house the next morning. A lot of relatives were there again. After a little while the men put their hats and jackets on and began to gather everyone together. I looked at my dad and asked, ''Where are we all going?''

He answered, ''We're going to see Grandpa.''

My heart leaped within me. I couldn't believe what I actually heard. I ran for my sweater. Inside I was saying, ''See, Gloria, it was just a dream. It's all okay, there's nothing to be scared about.'' With my heart beating until I could feel it pounding right through my little flowered spring dress, I ran as fast as I could to our car. I wanted to be the first one to see Grandpa. I needed him more than ever now. I wanted him to hold me and say, ''I love you, honey!''

We drove across town and parked on Main Street in front of a small, apricot-colored stucco building. I'd never been there before. All the relatives were gathering on the sidewalk. I couldn't understand their lack of concern after not seeing Grandpa for a whole day, so I ran in ahead.

I came to a big room with chairs all lined up. My eyes followed the aisle between the chairs, and then fell upon something I had never seen before. Way up in the front of this room was a beautiful long, shiny, reddish-brown box. It was rounded on both ends and it had a beautiful dark red velvet curtain draped around the bottom. The box was resting on little wheels. I looked up and the right half of the box was closed and the left half of the box was open. There was a creamy sheer curtain hanging down from the top of the cover that looked like a tent.

I was intrigued. No one was coming yet so I wandered down the aisle. The closer I came to this fancy box it looked as if someone was lying in it. I bravely walked right up to it—and my heart almost stopped. It was my *Grandpa!* What was he doing?

I thought, "He must be sleeping again." I cautiously moved my hand on the edge of the shiny box and edged my finger under the sheer curtain, sliding it over the creamy fancy satin until I could almost reach the shoulder of his pin-striped suit. I was scared and shaking, but I had to talk to him. I knew I had to wake him up. I tapped him on the shoulder and whispered, "Grandpa, you've got to wake up now!"

Just then someone pulled me back and scolded, "Don't touch him!!"

I looked into my uncle's face thinking, "What do you mean? You don't care about him! I love him, I know I can wake him up. He'll get up and everything will be O.K."

When my uncle turned away, I approached Grandpa again. But just as I was about to tap his shoulder, something dawned on me. Grandpa was so quiet. I'd never seen him sleep so hard. The urge to wake him up raged within me. "Grandpa, you have to wake up—you just have to!"

I felt a jerk on my long blonde hair pulling me back. Then came the most crushing words I had ever heard. "He's dead—he will never, ever talk to you again!"

Pains seized my chest. My head throbbed and I began to cry. I clung to the coffin that held the person I dearly loved. The words rang in my ears, "He's gone. He'll never talk to you again." I stood by the coffin and looked into the quiet, pale face of my grandfather. I felt as if a part of myself had died, too.

As this whole scene was being relived in my mind, do you know what the Lord focused my eyes upon? He showed me a spray of roses that were on each side of my Grandpa's coffin. The Lord began to minister to my heart. "Gloria, you don't hate roses. You have hated what the roses reminded you of. It reminded you of your grandfather's funeral. You really have hated Me. All these years you have blamed Me for taking away your grandfather, when you needed and loved him so much. You felt cheated of your grandfather's love. Gloria, you must release the bitterness you have harboured against Me so that I may be able to bless you and use you as you've desired to be used. Let Me take a spiritual eraser and remove all your pain and memories of that past event and let Me fill you with My blessing."

The Lord began to show me how this whole experience affected my life. I had nightmares for years after my grandfather died. (I always had to have a light on in my room at night because when it was dark, I visualized Grandpa's casket by my bed.)

Right then I cried, "Oh, God, I'm so sorry! Lord, I release all of it! Thank you, Lord, for bringing out of my subconscious all this sludge that has muddied and clogged my life. Now, Lord, I ask you to cleanse my heart—make it clean again."

About two weeks later Larry came bounding into the room holding a vase with a beautiful rose in it. He handed it to me proudly. I picked it up and smelled it. For the first time since we were married I looked up at him and said, "Oh, honey, I love it! I love the smell!"

From that moment on the rose has been a symbol of love to me. It is beautiful. All the hurts and scars are gone from this tragedy in my life. God had healed me. Now this gal *loves* roses!

5

Bologna Knees

*A*fter releasing my bitterness against death, roses and God, I felt so relieved. I couldn't believe that inner healing could make such a difference in my life—physically, emotionally and spiritually. For the first time in years I felt a new sense of the nearness of God and a new touch of His blessing on my life.

At the next two seminars I saw God working in the lives of our guests, and I felt like a bystander watching God speak through me—it was so exciting! When I was finished I'd say, "Wow, Lord, You really did a great job! All I had to do was stand there with the microphone and You did all the talking." I felt like a puppet in the hands of a master puppeteer.

I was so excited after the second seminar as we headed back for Minnesota I kept saying to God, "Wow, this is great! If this is what inner healing does for a person and his ministry, Lord, keep cleaning out the clogged pipes that have been stopped up in me. And, Lord, if there's anything else buried in my sub-conscious, keeping me from further blessings, tell me."

Again I heard the same concerned Voice filled with love speak to me, "Gloria, do you really love Me?"

"Oh, yes, Lord! I love You!"

"Do you really want Me to bless your life?"

"Oh, yes, Lord, please bless me! Lord, bless my life!"

Then, just like a father with a stern voice, yet clothed in love, He said, "Go ask Larry for forgiveness— you're bitter against him."

I began to laugh out loud. "O.K. God, maybe You were right the last time about bitterness against death and You, but this time You've got the wrong person. God, I love him. We have a neat relationship. We communicate, we have so much fun together. I know there isn't such a thing as a perfect marriage, but if there's a nearly perfect one, it's ours. So there!"

Then, just as if someone jolted me with 220 volts of electricity, I quickly sobered. "Oh-oh. Maybe there is something way down in my subconscious that I've forgotten. Here we go again. O.K., God, before I say there is definitely *no* bitterness against Larry, I guess I should pray and ask You to release any junk from my memory that may have been buried and forgotten."

I began thinking back through the previous few days and weeks and I couldn't come up with anything. Again I assured God, "Like I said, Lord, there's nothing to ask forgiveness for. I love him—do You hear? I'm not bitter against him—I love him."

Guess what? No sooner had I released those words when the Lord brought back out of my memory a whole event of my life I had totally forgotten.

The Newlywed Game

It was 1965, New Year's Eve in Pampa, Texas. I was

a bride of three months. The event was a big New Year's Eve service at a large church. Just like on a multi-media screen I saw myself standing in the big fellowship hall of the church. Larry and I were visiting with everyone—meeting new people and renewing old friendships Larry had made while visiting that church years ago.

We mingled with the crowd. Larry was greeted by several young couples who had gotten married since Larry last saw them. We all introduced ourselves and talked about where they had met and dated. Then one of the fellows turned to Larry, hit him in the arm and quipped, "Well, Larry, I see you finally bit the dust—you finally gave in and got married!"

"Well," asked one young man, "Where's Gloria from?" Larry ignored him. Again the man said, "Hey, where's Gloria from?"

Larry mumbled under his breath, "Um, mmm, mm, uh, South Dakota."

I'm thinking to myself, "Good grief Larry, speak up, tell them—South Dakota!"

Just as I thought that, he said, a little louder than before, "South Dakota."

They all began to laugh, point their fingers at him, joshing and joking. "You mean to tell us, after what you said about never marrying a girl from your home state or home town, you ended up marrying a girl from South Dakota?" they chided. And then they asked, "What town is she from?"

Larry blushed, shuffled his feet back and forth and sheepishly replied, "Sisseton."

"Where?" they questioned in disbelief.

"I said, Sisseton."

They all began to laugh again. Meanwhile I'm

thinking, "What's so funny about being from South Dakota? What's so hilarious about being from Sisseton? I am Gloria Brooks from Sisseton, South Dakota. I can't see anything so funny about that. There must be something here I don't know about. Oh well, no big deal."

Then I heard Larry say, "Yeah, I married Gloria Brooks even though she had *bologna knees*."

I couldn't believe my ears—the words boomeranged in my ears. Bologna knees! Then I screamed inside, "Bologna knees, eh? That *creep!* If I had known that was what he thought of me before we were married, I wouldn't have married him!"

Isn't that strange? Just two minutes before I had loved him with all my heart. Now he was a creep in my eyes. Love had turned into hate. You read me right—it wasn't just disgust, dislike or being peeved—I now *hated* him. It happened so quickly. After a few moments I somehow managed to excuse myself and returned to the motel.

After all this was relived the Lord stopped the flashback and said, "Gloria, you need to go ask Larry for forgiveness!"

I retorted, "What do you mean? *He's* the one who said I had bologna knees. *He's* the one who should come crawling on his knees and ask me for forgiveness."

Very politely and tenderly, the Lord continued, "Gloria, you go ask Larry for forgiveness. You're the one who's been hurting and bitter about it. He doesn't even remember what he said."

Oh, did that ever get my blood running hot! I said, "Listen, Lord, *You reminded me;* You can remind *him!*" Sounded sensible, didn't it?

Again God said, "What's My blessing worth in your

life? What's it worth?''

I began to mellow. "Oh, Lord, I'm sorry. I want Your blessing in my life more than anything in the whole world.''

Then, as if a giant unseen finger was pointed at me, I heard Him say, "Then you go ask Larry for forgiveness ...now!''

"No, no I won't. He wronged me.'' Oh, how my personal pride sprang up; resentment followed quickly. You see, I've always had the whole thing figured out. If someone wronged me or offended me, I'd say, "Go get 'em, God, make them miserable! Just manage it that everything will go wrong for them today. Then, Lord, when they are so miserable and my revenge has been satisfied, You force them to come crawling to me on their knees. When they finally ask for forgiveness, I'll respond, "Oh, I'll see if I feel like it.''

Ha! Come on now, all you who are reading this, you know what I'm talking about. I know you can identify with that. Take your mask off, let's be honest!

The verses in Matthew 6:12, 14-15 (TLB) began to come to my mind. I've read and prayed the Lord's prayer over hundreds of times in my lifetime, but now verse 12 began to jab me, *"...and forgive us our sins just as we have forgiven those who have sinned against us.''* Verses 14 and 15 set my heart pounding. *"Your Heavenly Father will forgive you if you forgive those who sin against you. But if you refuse to forgive them, He will not forgive you.''*

Then the Lord said, "Gloria, to forgive means to love. To forgive means to bless. Forgive him, Gloria, and I will bless you!''

Oh, how I wanted God's blessing. I thought, "There must be some easier way I can get that blessing without

43

having to go to Larry and forgive him—I'll figure out a way!'' But the bitterness began to rage even more. I felt like screaming and hollering at Larry. Then I had another flashback.

Gloria vs. Mom and God

A few days before we were to be married in October, 1965, my mother took me aside for one of our dozens of cherished, intimate sharing times. With a sweet but stern look on her face she announced, "Missy, I want to give you some golden advice. You know you'll be living in the public eye. You'll be living in a bus with six or eight other people. Things won't always go perfectly and you'll have some bad days, but this advice will keep you out of lots of trouble. Here it is—learn to keep your mouth shut! Don't say anything you would later regret."

I thought, "Well, I'd better apply that advice, but I'll go further than that." I decided I wouldn't talk to Larry, *period*. I had a feeling that if I opened my mouth I'd say more than I should, so I pulled away. The next three or four days I evaded him. I tried to be away when he'd wake up; I stayed totally out of his sight. I didn't want anything to do with him!

The Lord kept prompting me, "Gloria, release the bitterness. Go forgive Larry."

Each time I'd rebel, "No! No, I don't have to. I don't want to. Why should I? You just talk to him about it." The more I fought it, the more miserable I became. I actually had a headache and stomach pains from being so upset. I hadn't smiled or laughed in four days. I couldn't stand myself yet I hung on because of my pride.

Enroute to Bemidji, Minnesota, for a Family Life

Seminar, I was going through my seminar notes and felt blocked at every direction I turned. I couldn't pray, couldn't feel the Spirit of God. I pleaded, "Oh, God, I can't go to this seminar feeling like this. I'll have to tell Lowell I can't speak at that session—someone else will have to do it."

I felt a sweet Spirit and heard the words, "Gloria, do you want Me to bless your session tomorrow? Do you want Me to bless and use you?"

I almost leaped straight up. I felt there was hope. Then the same Voice with that big, invisible finger pointing lovingly commanded, "Go, ask Larry for forgiveness."

I sank back into my pillow. I said, "Oh, God, why are You doing this to me?" I turned to the alarm clock on my left. The ticking was adding tension to the whole ordeal. The clock read 3:30—it sounded like a time bomb ticking away its last few minutes. I cried, "Oh, God, You have to help me. I can't stand this anymore...."

Then, just as if I was shot out of a cannon, I found myself running down the aisle of the bus, plopped into the buddy seat next to Larry and scared him half to death! He almost let go of the steering wheel! Then a winning smile swept across his face as he greeted me. "Well, what a pleasant surprise! I felt so alone up here...." His eyes caught a glimpse of my face as the moon shone through the window. My face looked like a prune that had been picked and dried a year earlier. My eyes were bloodshot and my countenance was anything but pleasant. The "vibes" he was receiving left a lot to be desired.

"Honey, are you sick?"

"No," I barked, my eyes set straight ahead.

"Are you sure you're not sick...?" he asked.

"Yes, I'm sure!" My body stiffened. I couldn't and wouldn't look at him.

Tenderly he whispered, "Honey, I really love you. You know, you really haven't been yourself these past four or five days. You're always so sweet, loving and happy, but lately you haven't talked; you've stayed away from me. Honey, tell me what's wrong. We've always been able to communicate and share our feelings. I love you so much. Have I hurt or offended you? If I have, I don't remember what I said or did...."

I'm sure he could feel the steam blowing out of my stack—and by the look on my face he knew he was involved somehow.

Cautiously, as if approaching a man-eating lion, he repeated, "Honey, I don't remember saying anything or doing anything wrong. If I did, could you tell me when I did it?"

"Thirteen years ago!"

He looked at me with disbelief. "You mean you've been mad at me for thirteen years??" He began laughing.

"Yeah," I retorted, "I just remembered it!"

He fell over the steering wheel with this hilarious case of laughter that made me furious. How dare he laugh at me in my terrible dilemma! He sobered just enough to ask, "Honey, what did I say?"

"I'll tell you." And I did. I said, "Do you remember what you told those people after they asked where I was from?"

"No, Gloria, I can't remember what I said 13 years ago."

"I'll tell you what you said. You said, 'Yeah, I married Gloria even though she had *bologna knees*!'"

46

He cracked up again. Trying to gain his composure, he said, "Did you really think I was serious when I said that?"

I sank back in the buddy seat, holding my breath. "You didn't mean it?"

"Of course not, honey, I was just kidding! I love you. I'm proud of you. I'd never do or say anything to hurt you."

I felt sick through my entire body. My mind was racing. Don't tell me for 13 years I've been in bondage to my anger toward Larry and let a wall grow between us—just because I couldn't go back and talk my problem over with him that New Year's Eve in 1965!

Then I thought, "Has this really affected me?" The Lord showed me it had. For 13 years I would not wear a bathing suit, shorts or anything that would reveal my knees. I wasn't going to give my husband another chance to look at me and think, "Bologna knees, bologna knees!" Larry would literally beg me to put a swimsuit on and go swimming, but I always had an excuse. I deliberately left it at home so he wouldn't see me in it and laugh at me. A few years earlier, Larry had given me a beautiful, fancy powder-blue shortie pajama set. I never wore it for fear of him looking at me thinking, "Oh, look at those ugly bologna knees!" Now he tells me he didn't mean that statement and I've kept myself in bondage for 13 years—not being able to be myself around my own husband! I wasn't able to dress to please him because of my own hang-ups!

I looked at Larry. He was waiting for my response. I ordered, "Larry, pull this bus over! The Lord told me if I want His blessings on my life I have to forgive you—even though you said it." (I wasn't being very

47

polite!)

In a few seconds the big forty-foot rig came to a complete halt. There was silence except for the purr of the old bus motor. My pride wanted to fight, but I knew it was now or never. I said, "Larry, forgive me for holding this against you for 13 years. It has kept me from being free around you. Please forgive me. I've been so miserable this week. I need to be free so I can feel God's blessing again."

Tenderly, he held my hands and we prayed. Immediately I felt a new surge of love for Larry enter my heart. When I said, "Amen," I felt like laughing, so I did! Larry looked at me with a puzzled but pleased expression. All I thought at that moment was, "Gloria, how stupid you were to ever let anything like that destroy your intimacy, your dress codes and your freedom with your own husband. How silly you've been!"

The old bus began rolling down that lonesome old highway again, but I was no longer lonely, angry or miserable. I felt like a teenager who had just fallen in love for the first time—I was free!

6

Acid of Anger

After being released through inner healing in my experiences with my grandfather and husband, the Lord began to show me where anger and bitterness had taken a deadly toll on my spiritual life. What I thought was discomfort was really anger. I found out that anger will destroy you from the inside out. Anger and bitterness are companions—you can't be angry without being bitter and you can't be bitter without being angry.

Dr. Charles Stanley, in a tape series entitled, "How to Handle Your Emotions*," defines *anger* as, "a sudden inner feeling of displeasure and antagonism toward what we assume to be an irritating factor. It can be an environmental situation or a person in our life—and soon that feeling begins to consume that person or factor." That really puts it in a nutshell.

*In Touch Ministries, P.O. Box 7900,
  Atlanta, Georgia 30357

An example of the power of anger is found in the Bible in the very first family. Cain brought an offering of fruit to the Lord and it was rejected. Then Abel presented his offering of his flock and the Bible says, *"The Lord had respect unto Abel and to his offering"* (Genesis 4:4). Anger entered Cain; then bitterness toward his brother. It wasn't long before Cain was consumed with anger. The Bible says, *"Cain rose up against Abel his brother, and slew him"* (Genesis 4:8). Cain killed Abel because of the giant of anger that got out of control in Cain's life.

Ephesians 4:26 (TLB) says, *"If you are angry, don't sin by nursing your grudge. Don't let the sun go down with you still angry—get over it quickly, for when you are angry you give a mighty foothold to the devil."*

People get angry basically for four reasons:

1. They can't have their own way.
2. They can't endure pain.
3. They are overcome by frustration and anxiety.
4. They feel injustice has been done to them or others.

When any of these four areas are tampered with in our lives, anger and bitterness surface. If we over-react, our control button flies off, throwing common sense, justice, love and understanding right out the window. This is usually followed by cutting words, screaming, fighting, broken spirits, hurt feelings, pouting—even physical harm and many times death.

Our prisons are filled with people who are there because they lost control of their temper. Anger surfaced and was given a free rein, leading to personal assault and murder. Only after they had committed the crime did most of these people feel a release of their anger.

There are four ways to deal with anger:

1. You can *repress* it by pretending it doesn't exist. Pride will try to convince you that nothing's wrong—but when that anger keeps you awake at night for weeks, months or even years, you know it does exist.

2. You can *suppress* it by pushing anger down. You know it is there but you try to hold it in. It won't work, though. It's just like holding a balloon under water—by pressure you can hold it, but you have to let go sometime. When it's released, watch out! It will fly out of your hands.

3. You can *express* it by cursing, screaming or cutting remarks, leaving scars on those to whom it has been expressed.

4. You can *give it to Christ*. This is the winning way to deal with anger and bitterness.

You must:

1. Confess your sin of anger.

2. Admit you need help and be willing to be helped.

3. Go to the one you are angry with and ask forgiveness. (*"Leave there thy gift before the altar, and go thy way; first be reconciled to thy brother, and then come and offer thy gift"* [Matthew 5:24]).

Friend, if you've been fighting the acid of anger in your life, you too can release it and be free. Please pray with me:

Lord, I admit I've been marred by the ugly acid of anger and I don't want to suppress or repress it anymore; it's eating me up. Right now, in the name

of Jesus, I express my desire to be released. I surren-
der my own sinful nature that has ignited these
explosions of anger. I ask You to fill me with Your
love, peace and patience. Thank you, Lord, Amen.

7

Relentless Rejection

*T*he weapon of rejection is one of the most brutal weapons anyone can use on someone else. It's used by husbands, wives, parents, brothers, sisters, sinners and Christians alike. We live in an environment of rejection and are surrounded by this deadly weapon. But I've been encouraged by Isaiah 54:17, *"No weapon that is formed against thee shall prosper."* You have power over the weapon of rejection even though it may already have been used on you.

First of all, where does rejection come from? Rejection is a wounded spirit that has its origin in the beginning of life. A child has the capacity to sense feelings in the womb.

Dr. Thomas Verny, a Canadian psychiatrist and one of the world's leading authorities on the unborn child, states in the *St. Paul Pioneer Press*, December 23, 1982:

In utero, they (unborn babies) know their mother's voices, and can feel her love—or her rejection.... What happens to babies before and during birth can create positive characteristics, or problems that remain with them the rest of their lives....

While a pregnant woman's occasional bouts with anxiety or ambiguous feelings are normal and harmless, continued personal stress or hostility toward the coming child often can produce a sickly, unhappy infant and a difficult delivery....

Studies also show that bonding after birth—mother and child cuddling, hugging, kissing and feeding—is important to the child's long-term well-being.

The early years make impressions in our minds that we will have to live with the rest of our lives. Parents can either make or break the child during those early years of life.

The following are examples from hundreds of letters that I have received since ministering through sessions about inner healing:

I feel so unwanted. My mother was pregnant before she got married, and she keeps telling me, 'If it hadn't been for you, I could have gone to college and become something. Now I'm just a mother.' I feel I've messed up her life.

Another writes:

Several times in my life my father has said to me, 'I wanted a son, and we got you.' This feeling of rejection haunts me every time he looks at me.

A teenager spoke up at a seminar and lamented, "One night at dinner after my dad had a hard day at work he said, 'Your mom and I had big plans to do things together and go places for enjoyment—then you shocked us and were born to us late in our lives. You've messed up all our plans!'"

These statements plant seeds of rejection in the lives of these young people and adults and they are disturbed by thoughts of "I'm a mistake," "I messed up their lives," "They wish I hadn't been born," "I just don't belong," "Where do I go?" Soon these people pull away and many of them become depressed, runaways, loners and even suicidal. If you know someone with these symptoms, more than likely they have been wounded by the weapon of rejection.

Some children need and demand more love and attention than others. Here's a letter from a college girl in North Dakota:

Gloria, my mother and I can't communicate anymore. I've been hurt. First of all, I guess I have to go back and tell you that I was a very insecure girl. I always felt rejected and unloved. So I always stayed very close to my mother, and hung tight to her. Two years ago we were at a family reunion and I was off playing baseball with some other relatives. I came back just in time to hear several of the adults laughing. When they saw me coming, they began pointing at me and laughing all the more. A relative chided, "Did you really do that?" I looked at them and said, "What did I do?" My mother looked at them and then looked at me and sarcastically remarked, "Oh, don't you remember, Susan? You always used to hang on me. I got so sick and tired of it—you always wanted to hold my hand, always had to have your arm around my neck. I'm so glad you've grown up and don't do that anymore." From that day on I never dared touch my mother. I no longer feel that she loves me and I feel rejected because she made fun of my insecure feelings.

Probably one of the most crushing experiences of rejection I've heard was at Winnipeg, Manitoba, Canada. I had asked for those who needed a prayer for inner healing to step forward and a petite, well-dressed brunette, who had been very poised throughout the whole seminar, let her mask fall as she burst into tears. "Please pray for me. I need a healing of rejection in my life. When I was 3 1/2 years old my mother bundled me up in my snowsuit and she and Daddy carried me out to the car on a cold, snowy day. We drove and drove and finally parked by a big building. They carried me up a long stairway, walked into a big room and then threw me into the arms of a complete stranger and commanded, 'Take her! We don't want her anymore.' They turned and quickly disappeared. I screamed and screamed, 'Daddy, Momma, please don't leave me! I love you. Please don't leave me—please! I love you!' I never saw them again.''

This lady, 40 years old, confessed, "I'm so scared. I even live in fear of my marriage, always thinking that some day my husband might leave me, too. It's so horrible!"

It's important that you analyze your feeling of rejection. Were you rejected as a person—or were your attitudes, actions or words rejected? There is a difference between being rejected because of who you are or because of something you did. Maybe you have felt rejection from childhood and you're wondering, "How can I overcome this feeling of rejection?" All of the people you just read about have had tragic experiences with rejection. Perhaps you also have had similar experiences. What is the solution to these problems?

1. Recognize the source—Where did this feeling come from? Realize this very important fact: it did not come from Christ! Jesus said, *"He that cometh to me I will in no wise cast out"* (John 6:37). Even though He was rejected of men, mistreated, bruised and beaten, the Lord said, *"I will never leave thee, nor forsake thee"* (Hebrews 13:5). That's a promise of God. Be comforted to know He never breaks His promises.

2. If you feel you were rejected or unwanted as a child, you must forgive those who hurt you. You must forgive them because they acted out of ignorance or against the will of God, or possibly because they did what they felt was right at the time. Colossians 3:13 says, *"Be gentle and ready to forgive; never hold grudges. Remember, the Lord forgave you, so you must forgive others"* (TLB).

Keep your own heart clean. Don't become bitter or resentful. Vengeance belongs to the Lord—not you (see Deuteronomy 32-35). Don't spend your life in tears, fears and regrets when you could be living life to its fullest.

If you're a sensitive person, maybe you feel your attitude, advice or position has been rejected. Maybe this won't comfort you any, but here it is in a nutshell—*that's life*. We are all going to face rejection at some time in our lives, so we must learn to accept it to a point—but we don't have to give in to it. Reject the rejection! We shouldn't take things so personally, and we should learn not to feel sorry for ourselves.

3. Build a relationship with Jesus Christ. You won't have to fear rejection if you realize you are of great value to the Father. He loves you!

A young man said to me, "No one loves me—no one cares."

I interrupted his song of rejection, "Hey! Wait a minute. I know three people who love you!"

His eyes got big. "Who?"

I looked at him and said, "One. God the Father—He cared enough that He created you. He would never create anything that had no value.

"Two. Jesus the Son loves you—He saved you by dying on the cross for you. He'd never suffer, bleed and die for someone He never cared for.

"Three. The Holy Spirit loves you—He would never spend His time working in your heart and mind to tell you the difference between right and wrong if He didn't love you. He wouldn't dwell in something that was not worth anything.

"So, there!" I finished. "They all love you!"

He responded, "Wow, I never thought of that!"

Now, how about you? Have you ever thought about that?

Feelings of rejection can cause us to reject ourselves, reject others and regretfully reject Jesus Christ, the only One who really knows, loves and understands us and our feelings. Jesus Christ is the only One who can heal those feelings of rejection. All we have to do is confess these feelings and then accept His acceptance of us as His child.

Are you willing to confess and accept His love? If so, pray with me right now:

Dear Heavenly Father,

I love You and thank You for loving me. Lord, I ask You to heal my damaged emotions. Forgive me for giving in to these feelings of rejection. Satan has kept me in bondage to them. Right now I release the hurts, scars, and bitterness I've harbored against all of those who have rejected me. Lord, I bless them right now.

Lord, I forgive my parents for not loving me and caring for me when I needed their attention so badly. Lord, I forgive my teachers, classmates, brothers, sisters and friends for rejecting me when I longed to feel involved and needed. Bless every one of them, Lord. Bless their lives.

Thank you, Jesus, right now for the inner healing that is taking place in my life. Thank You for healing the hurts, scars and memories and filling me with Your great love! Oh, thank you, Jesus! Thank you, Father and thank you, Holy Spirit for loving me and being so very patient with me! In Jesus' name I pray, Amen.

8

Freedom From Fear

or God hath not given us the spirit of fear; but of power, and of love, and of a sound mind" (2 Timothy 1:7). Even though we have this promise in the Bible, fear still keeps Christians from God's blessings in their lives. If Satan can implant fear within people, he soon can rule them through those fears.

When fear begins to enter our hearts and minds we begin to panic. The only way to get rid of fear is to hold on to God's promises as given to us in the Bible.

The following is one of the most exciting testimonies I've ever heard concerning the power of holding on to God's promises. This is a true story. It was related to me by a very dear friend, Julie Carter, from Decorah, Iowa, who has now gone to be with the Lord.

Promise With Power

One summer day in 1978, Julie's friend, Jan*, in California attended a Bible study with another friend, Bonnie.* The Scripture shared that day was Psalm 46:1 and 2, *"God is our refuge and strength, a tested help in times of trouble"* (TLB).

---

*Names have been changed.

On the way home they decided to spend a few minutes at a large shopping mall. When they returned to Jan's new car, they saw four or five young men loitering around it. The ladies quickly walked through the gang, jumped into the car, rolled up the windows and locked the doors. Then the men began to terrorize them by beating on the car and pulling on the door handles. Bonnie stated that fear gripped both of them and they began to imagine what the men would do if they broke in. Jan tried to start the car but to no avail. She tried again and it still wouldn't start.

She turned to Bonnie and said, "We've never had any problems with this car—it's almost new. I don't know why it won't start."

Bonnie, alarmed, said, "Jan, we don't have time to waste. Let's test the verses we learned." She began to repeat the words, "God is our refuge and strength, a tested help in times of trouble." Then she prayed, "O.K. God, in Jesus' name, we're standing on your Word."

Jan then turned the key and the car started up immediately. She slowly forced her way through the angry young men. Looking in the rearview mirror as she sped off, she saw the men staring at their car in disbelief.

She drove home as quickly as she could, pulled into the driveway, jumped out and ran into the arms of her husband and began sobbing out her story.

He consoled her and then exclaimed, "That's a new car! You shouldn't have had any problems starting it."

She cried, "Believe me, honey, it wouldn't start. Then, after we repeated Psalm 46:1 and 2, about God being our refuge and strength in times of trouble, I breathed the name of Jesus, turned the key, and the car started right off.''

After calming her down, Jan's husband explained he was going to check the car. In a few moments he returned, his face pale and bewildered. ''Jan, honey, no wonder the car wouldn't start—the battery's gone! There's no battery in the car, Jan. Those men took it.''

They both cried and praised God, for they *knew* God had performed a miracle before their very eyes. Jan knew that miracle took place because she put the promises of God in action. *''God is my refuge and strength, a tested help in times of trouble.''* You can draw upon the power of God's promises to help you overcome fear.

The Force of Fear

There are two types of fear. One is a natural fear that God puts within you to protect you. Why do you fear a raging lion or a rattlesnake? Because if you didn't have some sense of fear, you'd walk right up to the lion and he'd maul you to death. Or maybe you'd go to pick up the rattlesnake to play with it and it would bite you and the poisonous venom would kill you. These are healthy fears. But then there are fears that the devil would throw upon you. Bad experiences that happen to you or to others build up a wall of fear that grip and control you in many areas of your life.

Every one of us have had experiences of one or more types of fear. Some fears that you have come in contact with have left you numb, weak, breathless, shaking, crying or hysterical. There are fears of sickness, disease, accidents, height, water, flying, swimming, doctors, needles, blood and many others. These are some of the fears that we come in contact with almost every day.

You may need inner healing for a number of these fears.

A few months ago I held a session in a convention hall in Eau Claire, Wisconsin. At the end of the session, I asked those who wanted to receive inner healing to come forward to receive prayer. Almost three hundred came forward.

Linda*, a meek-spirited teenager, walked up to me and cried, "Gloria, please pray for me. I have a fear of water."

I asked, "Do you know why you have a fear of water?"

She said, "No, I don't have any idea. I've been praying about it. I've been asking God to bring out of my subconscious the reason why I'm scared of water, but I just don't know. Please pray for me, because this fear hinders my life. I can't even go out and have any fun."

"Let's pray right now," I suggested. "Let's pray that the Lord will reveal the truth." We prayed, and after we finished, she just stood there with a blank look on her face. I asked, "Did the Lord show you anything?"

She shook her head and said, "No, I don't remember anything." She seemed to be confused. I told her that I would be praying for her and that I wanted to talk to her privately after the service.

I dismissed the service and was counseling with several people when a stately-looking woman walked up to me. I could sense the Spirit of God upon her.

"Gloria, may I speak with you a moment?" she asked politely.

---

*Not her real name..

"Sure."

"I was sitting over on the left side of the auditorium and the Lord spoke to me. He showed me what has happened to that girl who was so afraid of water." That statement interested me because I had felt such a heavy burden for this young girl. She continued, "Gloria, when Linda was seven months old her mother was bathing her and accidentally dropped her into a deep tub of water. It frightened her then, and she still fears water."

I was so excited. I touched the woman's shoulder and said, "Thank you for sharing what God laid on your heart. I want to find Linda and tell her what you said."

My heart was overwhelmed to know that God cared so much about Linda's need. I was anxious to share this with her and I looked everywhere for her, but I couldn't find her. My heart sank.

The auditorium was empty and we were just moving the last few pieces of equipment out the door when, to my surprise, I ran into Linda! "Oh, Gloria, I just came to thank you...well, I guess I came to apologize for being so silly by asking you to pray for my fear of water when there's so many people with more desperate needs than mine."

I hugged her! "Oh, I'm so happy to see you. Come here! May I speak with you a moment?"

We found a quiet corner. My heart was throbbing with joy. I asked her, "Do you believe that God speaks to people's hearts?"

"Yes!"

I asked another question, "Linda, do you believe that God cares about you? Do you believe that He's concerned as to why you have a fear of water?"

"Oh yes," she responded.

Then I told her how the Lord spoke to another Christian woman and showed her why Linda had a fear of water.

Impatiently Linda said, "Oh, please, please tell me!"

"Listen carefully. The Lord told her that when you were seven months old, your mother was bathing you and she accidentally dropped you into a deep tub of water and it scared you. That fear has kept you in bondage ever since."

She laughed a sigh of relief and said, "Well, no wonder I couldn't remember, no wonder!" Her eyes got big and then panic covered her pretty face. She said, "Oh! Do you know what happened today?"

"No, I don't."

"My girlfriend and I were babysitting a seven-month old baby at a swimming pool, and my girlfriend accidentally dropped the baby into the water. And that baby screamed hysterically. But, Gloria, now it all makes sense. Now I know why the Lord wanted to heal me tonight! I've got to go back and pray for this baby and ask God to release the fear and erase the memory from this baby's mind. Otherwise, she will grow up with the same fear I've been carrying all these years."

I prayed with her. She looked at me with the most peaceful shine on her face. "Gloria, it's gone," she said. "My fear of water is gone! I'm free! God has healed me."

God doesn't want you to be in bondage. He wants you to be free.

Fear Takes Over

One of the leading fears among people today is the fear of public speaking. Satan knows if we won't get up to speak, he can keep us from being used in a public ministry witnessing to others.

This became real to me about seven years ago in Benson, Minnesota. I was asked to speak at a country club luncheon. I prayed about it and felt the Lord urging me to do it. I was excited about sharing.

All went smoothly, so I thought, until afterward when a brassy woman briskly walked up to me and blurted, "You offended me." I was taken aback.

I said, "Pardon me?"

She said, in a thundering voice, "You offended me. I did not like that one statement you said."

I asked her what I'd said, and she quickly told me! I felt she had misinterpreted my statement, but I said, "I'm sorry. I really didn't mean to offend you." A few minutes later I retreated to the bus and broke down crying. "Lord, I'm sorry. I didn't mean to hurt that lady's feelings. I was only sharing to be a blessing to other people. Lord, because I made a mistake and I guess I offended some people, I just won't speak anymore."

I called our coordinator and quickly commanded, "Don't book any more speaking engagements for me. Please! Just tell them that I'm not available." But inside I was crying—frustrated and hurt. I didn't want to embarrass God. I didn't want to be a failure to Him anymore.

After several months of not speaking in public, I became miserable. I knew the only way I could be happy was to be ministering. I felt stagnant.

The Lord urged, "Gloria, if you want to be happy, you have to share."

Again I said, "Lord, how can I do it? Lord, I embarrassed You...I made a fool out of myself. I'm sorry."

Then the devil began intimidating me. He said to me, "Who do you think you are? You're no speaker. You're no singer. You don't use correct English. You're making a fool of yourself." I was devastated.

A few nights later I spent several hours in intense prayer. Exhausted, I fell asleep. The Lord interrupted my sleep and asked, "Gloria, do you know why you fear speaking? Do you know why you fear being up in front of big crowds?"

Though I was sleepy I said, "Oh, Lord, p-l-e-a-s-e tell me...why do I fear it?"

Tenderly and lovingly He answered, "Because you are trying to sell Gloria. You're worrying about Gloria and what Gloria's going to say!" Right in front of my eyes, in big block letters on the wall I saw my name: **G-L-O-R-I-A**.

The Lord spoke again. "Gloria, if you will drop the letters of your name on these blocks and replace them with the same number of letters, **C-H-R-I-S-T**, all your fears will leave, because I will speak through you."

I was so overwhelmed by His powerful words that I totally surrendered. I said, "O.K., Lord, I'm through worrying about Gloria, I'm through selling Gloria. I won't worry about my feelings, Lord, as long as I know You will speak through me."

Praise God, from that day on, as long as I pray and ask God for His Holy Spirit to lead me—as long as I know what I'm saying is what the Lord wants me to say—I no longer have a fear of speaking in public.

Has Satan kept you trapped by fears in your everyday life like he has to me and others? If you're tired of these fears limiting your lifestyle, goals, and relationship to God, pray with me and ask the Lord to set you free.

Heavenly Father, I rebuke Satan and his tactics for keeping me bound in fear. In the name of Jesus, I can face my fears, realizing You will release its grip. I accept the peace and confidence to achieve the tasks and goals set before me. Let me realize that You are one step ahead of me, leading the way—I don't have to fear anymore. I love You, Lord, Amen.

These verses will help you in your battle against the power of fear. Tear them out and place them where you will see them every day. Try to memorize them and use them as your shield of protection when Satan attacks you with fear.

Exodus 14:13 (TLB)—*"Don't be afraid. Just stand where you are and watch, and you will see the wonderful way the Lord will rescue you today."*

Deuteronomy 31:8 (TLB)—*"Don't be afraid, for the Lord will go before you and will be with you; he will not fail nor forsake you."*

Psalm 27:1 (TLB)—*"The Lord is my light and my salvation; whom shall I fear?"*

Psalm 46:1,2 (TLB)—*"God is our refuge and strength, a tested help in times of trouble. And so we need not fear even if the world blows up, and the mountains crumble into the sea."*

Psalm 91:5 (TLB)—*"Now you don't need to be afraid of the dark any more, nor fear the dangers of the day."*

Psalm 56:10,11 (TLB)—*"I am trusting God—oh, praise his promises! I am not afraid of anything mere man can do to me! Yes, praise his promises."*

Psalm 112:7 (TLB)—*"He does not fear bad news, nor live in dread of what may happen. For he is settled in his mind that Jehovah will take care of him."*

Psalm 118:6 (KJV)—*"The Lord is on my side; I will not fear: what can man do unto me?"*

Psalm 121:6-8 (KJV)—*"The sun shall not smite thee by day, nor the moon by night. The Lord shall preserve thee from all evil: he shall preserve thy soul. The Lord shall preserve thy going out and thy coming in from this time forth, and even for evermore."*

Proverbs 1:33 (TLB)—*"But all who listen to me shall live in peace and safety, unafraid."*

Isaiah 12:2 (TLB)—*"...I will trust and not be afraid, for the Lord is my strength and song; he is my salvation."*

Isaiah 35:4 (TLB)—*"Encourage those who are afraid. Tell them, 'Be strong, fear not, for your God is coming to destroy your enemies. He is coming to save you.'"*

Isaiah 41:10 (TLB)—*"Fear not, for I am with you. Do not be dismayed. I am your God. I will strengthen you; I will help you; I will uphold you with my victorious right hand."*

Isaiah 41:13 (TLB)—*"I am holding you by your right hand—I, the Lord your God—and I say to you, Don't be afraid; I am here to help you."*

Isaiah 43:2-4 (TLB)—*"When you go through deep waters and great trouble, I will be with you. When you go through rivers of difficulty, you will not drown! When you walk through the fire of oppression, you will not be burned up—the flames will not consume you. For I am the Lord your God, your Savior…you are precious to me and honored, and I love you."*

Luke 12:32 (TLB)—*"So don't be afraid, little flock…."*

John 14:27 (KJV)—*"Peace I leave with you, my peace I give unto you: not as the world giveth, give I unto you. Let not your heart be troubled, neither let it be afraid."*

2 Timothy 1:7 (KJV)—*"For God hath not given us the spirit of fear; but of power, and of love, and of a sound mind."*

Hebrews 13:6 (TLB)—*"That is why we can say without any doubt or fear, 'The Lord is my Helper and I am not afraid of anything that mere man can do to me!'"*

1 John 4:18 (KJV)—*"There is no fear in love; but perfect love casteth out fear: because fear hath torment. He that feareth is not made perfect in love."*

9

Injury of Incest

*I*f you have been crushed through a terrible experience of incest—you're hurting; you may feel guilty and dirty. This experience may have affected your whole life and relationships with others. I want to help release you from this pit of bondage and lift you into a new world of freedom. Otherwise you will be scarred for the rest of your life emotionally, mentally, physically and spiritually.

I want you to pray right now and ask God to keep your heart and mind open to what you will be reading and experiencing in this chapter.

Dear Lord, as I read this chapter on incest, I pray that You will give me the courage to face the truths You will be teaching me. Let me feel Your love and support as I put aside my reluctance to face these issues. Thank You, Lord, Amen.

My heart was grieved at the shocking statistics stating that one out of three females (women, teenagers and little girls) have been scarred by incest. Not only women and girls, but also men and boys have not escaped this plague. According to Dr. Judith Herman, a psychiatrist and the medical director of the Women's Mental Health Collective in Somerville, Massachusetts:

> Between a fourth and a third of all girls are sexually approached by an adult male, and about 10 percent have a sexual encounter with a relative. At least 1 percent become involved in father-daughter incest.
>
> Father-daughter incest is the most frequently reported form of sexual abuse within the family and has great potential for long-lasting harm to the child.

Until recent years incest has been a "hush" subject. But because guilt has eaten away at these victims, they are finally coming into the open to express their feelings and share their stories.

Hurting People

Dear Gloria,

Please pray that I can be healed of the guilt I've carried in my life for years. My father sexually molested me until I was 15 years old, when he died. But I'm still filled with revenge. Even though I know he's dead, if I could kill him again and again it wouldn't be enough to repay all the feelings of embarrassment and hurt he has caused me and our marriage. I hate him, and I'm filled with guilt. How can I release these feelings?

—Billings, MT

Dear Gloria,

I'm the wife of a policeman. You "hit home" when you talked about incest in your seminar. I was an

76

incest victim of my father and it ruined my first marriage. I wouldn't let my husband touch me because of the memories I had of my experiences with my father, so we divorced and I'm married again. But it's also destroying my second marriage. I haven't told my husband the reasons why I keep rejecting him because I'm afraid he'd kill my father. My father keeps calling us long-distance and inviting our 13-year-old daughter to come and spend a few days with him, but I won't let her go. I haven't had the heart to tell her why. I'm scared of him and I'm scared for my daughter. He says he's changed, but how do I really know? How do I forgive him? How do I forget those memories that plague me every time I get in bed with my husband?

—Des Moines, IA

Dear Gloria,

I attended your seminar in Bismarck, North Dakota, and it really became apparent to me that I needed inner healing.

When I was growing up at home, my father sexually abused me. I couldn't tell anyone because we lived in a small community and the word would have spread like wildfire. You see, my dad is an elder in the church and appears to be a spiritual leader. I didn't want my mom to find out because I knew it would deeply hurt her.

It's all over now. It happened ten years ago, but I still need to be healed of the memory. I don't think a day goes by that the devil doesn't bring it to my attention.

—P.T., North Dakota

Dear Gloria,

What you shared at the seminar last weekend brought back pictures of what my dad and grandfather did to me. They both sexually abused me. I couldn't say anything to my mother because Dad had a bad heart and said if I told anyone he might have a heart attack and die. So I wrote it all down in a diary. One day after my dad died, my mother found it and read about the experiences. She said she didn't believe it or me. That really hurt.

Then as a teenager I got pregnant from a boy I was dating. We married, but I hated him and I hated my new baby because she looked just like him. He physically and mentally abused me so I divorced him, and later had another child out of wedlock. I didn't care about anything anymore, not even my two baby girls....

Dear Gloria,

On September 20 I took a large bottle of Tylenol and swallowed the entire contents. I wanted to end my life, but for some reason God wouldn't allow it to happen. Help came to me in time. This suicide attempt was a result of marital problems and sexual abuse from my dad when I was a little girl. My dad "proclaimed" to be a Southern Baptist preacher, but he surely didn't live it. During your Set Free session the Lord showed me that the resentment I've had for my father has kept me from God and His blessings. All these years I've felt so dirty and so unclean. When I lived at home I ate and I ate, hoping to become so fat and ugly that my father wouldn't desire my body, but it didn't work. Finally, I ran away from home and married just to get away from him, only to find that my experience with my dad destroyed my marriage.

My father also sexually abused my two sisters. I told Mom, but she loved Dad so much she was afraid they'd get a divorce, so she never did anything about it.

—Omaha, NE

In comparing these and other letters, they all seem to follow a pattern. Most of the women were molested as children by a grandfather, father, uncle or acquaintance. They've all experienced fear, anguish, embarrassment and guilt that clung to them since the very first time they were victimized. Many of the women were threatened never to tell anybody or they would be physically harmed or tormented.

So, unfortunately, the victims became prisoners—not only to the person they were involved with, but also to fear and guilt.

I was a guest speaker at a luncheon held at a big Baptist church in Pueblo, Colorado, some time ago. The Lord blessed and at the close of the session 125 ladies stood to receive inner healing.

I recall the heavy burden the Lord laid on my heart when I began to speak on incest. The Lord revealed that a large number of those attending had been victims. After the session I counseled many ladies and young women. As I was leaving the church through the parking lot, I heard someone beckoning me with a tone of frustration in her voice. I turned around and my eyes fell upon a girl about 26 years old, around five feet tall with blonde hair and blue eyes. As she neared me, I noticed that she had been critically burned some time previously. Evidently she had had plastic surgery performed on her face, but from the neck down she was a mass of scar tissue. As my eyes met hers, they filled with tears and pain. "Gloria, do you really believe those people who molest girls and boys are really mentally and emotionally sick or do you think they are just plain 'jerks'?"

I re-emphasized what I had said earlier in the session. "If a man or woman is controlled by God in his heart and life, he or she wouldn't do that, but if he's controlled by a spirit of Satan, he's mentally, emotionally and spiritually sick. He or she needs to be set free by the power of God to break the strongholds of Satan on his life."

Nonchalantly she answered, "O.K., good-bye now," and began walking in the opposite direction.

The Lord prompted me, "Go talk to her." I quickly turned around and called out, "Miss, oh Miss." She turned back with tear-stained eyes. I commanded, "No matter what, never let it happen to you."

She tearfully confessed, "It already has."

My heart sank. I put my arm around her.

She began shaking and said, "My whole family—my mom, dad and my two brothers. They all did it to me— so I moved away from home. My mom was a lesbian. My dad and brothers sexually molested me. I hate them all for hurting me."

This poor young woman was not only in bondage to her whole family, but ran in fear of both men and women. She didn't trust anyone, so she lived the life of a loner. Many emotionally handicapped children and adults, unable to protect themselves, have been taken advantage of, like this girl.

A few months ago after a seminar in Milwaukee, Wisconsin, a frail but nice-looking woman approached me. She had long flowing dark brown hair, big brown eyes, and a tiny voice that accented her meek personality. She was shaking so uncontrollably that I put my arm around her to comfort her while she cried out her story.

"Gloria, my husband was killed in a car accident two years ago, and now there is just me, my daughter and a son. Please pray for my daughter, Michelle. She's 14 years old and she needs a miracle of God. She's in another state in a hospital suffering from a nervous breakdown. She had run away from home about six weeks ago and I've been nearly hysterical ever since. Two weeks ago the police called and ordered me to go immediately to the hospital where they had found her. When I arrived, I was ushered into her room. I ran over to her, held her closely, and questioned, 'Michelle, honey, why did you run away from home? I love you. I've been so worried about you. Everything's O.K. now, let's go back home. Please tell me, why did you run away?' She lay there, oblivious to what I said. She didn't answer me. After a few hours she finally broke down crying, 'Mom, I can't go home. You have to understand. I can't go home.' Then she began sobbing again. I tried to console her, but to no avail. A few days later when she was feeling better, she finally opened up and said, 'Mom, you know that nice guy you met at church and you've been dating for the past year?' I acknowledged, 'Yes.'

"She continued, 'Well, Mom, I know you like him and I know you've appreciated him coming over and doing chores for you, and I know you've appreciated him babysitting me free of charge so you wouldn't have to hire a babysitter when you worked at nights, but...' she hesitated, then began sobbing again, 'Oh, Mom,

I'm sorry, but I just have to tell you this. Do you know that almost every night since he started coming over to take care of me, he has locked the doors, taken me to the back bedroom and raped me? It hurt so much; I feel so dirty; I feel so guilty. I told him I was going to tell you and he threatened me that if I told anyone he'd kill me. Oh, Mom, I'm so scared. I had no choice. I had to run away.'''

Stories like this one have been told to me by scores of women and teenagers—boys, girls, even children.

I want to give a word of caution at this time to parents who hire babysitters. Be careful of whom you hire to watch your children. Be sure you know them—I mean *really* know them, or you may have things going on under your roof that you've never even thought of.

Question your children. Ask them if the babysitters, brothers, uncles or father have ever tried to sexually molest them or fondle their bodies. Assure them they will be protected and that nothing will happen to them if they tell you. They may be just waiting to get rid of the guilt of incest.

Innocent Guilt

The first dart that Satan throws at an incest victim is guilt. He fills the conscious and subconscious mind with the thoughts, "I'm no good," "I'm dirty," "I've been used," "I'm no longer pure." But these are all lies from the pits of hell. You don't have to carry the guilt. You're not guilty of the act, you were forced into it. You are only guilty if you willfully made the decision to be a part of the act. Whether you are guilty or not, you can be set free.

There are two steps you can take to be healed in the area of incest.

1. Determine whether you were guilty of the act or not. If you were, ask God to forgive you. 1 John 1:9 says, *"If we confess our sins, He is faithful and just to forgive us our sins,* (whether they are sexual or other kinds of sin) *and to cleanse us from all unrighteousness."* He has promised to forgive us and cleanse us. So after confessing our sin, we are forgiven—clean and pure again in God's sight. Just accept your forgiveness as a free gift from Christ Jesus.

   If you know you were forced into the sex act, then you're not guilty; it is as simple as that. When Satan tries to make you feel guilty, don't listen to him. Just say right out loud, "Satan, you're a liar, and I won't accept guilt feelings any more. I'm clean through Jesus' blood. I am innocent; I don't have to accept your lies." Then believe it.

2. The key to being healed from the experience of incest is to forgive the person who sexually abused you. I can just hear you say, "What do you mean, forgive him? He hurt and scarred me. I hate him. I wish he were dead for what he did." Believe me, forgiveness is essential for God to begin an inner healing in your life. In ourselves, in the human state of mind, we cannot and will not forgive, but through Jesus Christ, He can give us the will to forgive.

Recently a mother of two little girls stopped me after a session in Fargo, North Dakota, and said, "Gloria, the Lord really spoke to my heart during your inner healing session about incest. I was a victim of my father. He began to fondle my body as a child, and when

I became a teenager he'd come into my bedroom and force sex with me. I hated it. Mom was away working. Finally, when I was 15 years old I ran away from home and got married to a complete stranger just so I couldn't be forced to go back home. But because of the memory of what my father did to me, I wouldn't let my husband hardly ever touch me. Finally, after a year and a half, he left me. I was still just a kid. I needed security and companionship. So I remarried—and then the same thing happened again. I wouldn't let my new husband touch me either. Soon he left. I married for the third time, and Gloria, my marriage is on the rocks again because of my past."

She went on, "I attended a family reunion a few months ago. I really didn't want to go because I knew my dad would be there, but I finally decided to. I tried to ignore him, but finally he walked over to me and kidded, 'Hey, Sherry*, do you remember what we used to do when you were a teenager?' My heart began pounding until I thought it would jump out of my chest. I said, 'Yes, I remember, and I hate you for it! You've ruined my whole life. Two marriages have fallen apart because of you!' He chuckled, 'Hey, don't be upset about it. All the guys I was working with at the time were doing it with their daughters.' I shouted, 'I hate you! I hate you! I hate you!'"

Then she said, "Gloria, help me. Please help me. How can I be healed of this hatred and of the memories?"

I put my arm around her to comfort her. "Sherry, of course you hate him. And you have a reason to hate him, but it doesn't solve your problem with him or your

---

*Name changed.

marriage. Hating is not the answer." I continued, "What if a man walked up to you here in the lobby yesterday and slapped you in the face or said some cutting remark to you? Of course you'd be angry or hateful. But then, what if this morning someone informed you that this man had been taken to the hospital for psychotherapy, and explained that that was the reason he'd acted so strangely? What leaped up within you yesterday as hatred would now turn into pity because you'd think, 'Oh, that poor man, he's emotionally ill, sick and disturbed, he doesn't know what he's doing. His actions have been controlled by this ailment. Oh, I forgive him. He's not responsible for his actions. He's so very sick.' The same concept is true in dealing with incest. No man or woman who is emotionally, physically, mentally and spiritually well would ever sexually abuse a child or young person, true? Then, that leaves only one conclusion—he or she is 'sick.'"

After praying with Sherry, she clasped my hands and smiled, "Gloria, I can't explain what has happened in the past few minutes during prayer, but I feel so clean. I feel so pure, and for the first time in my life I feel love, a God-given love for my father. Oh, praise God, I'm free."

Jesus said, *"You shall know the truth, and the truth shall set you free"* (John 8:32). In the Bible in John 8:36 it says, *"If the Son therefore shall make you free, you shall be free indeed."* No matter what you've done, the Lord can set you free. Never think you've gone too far or have been too bad. God is here right now and He's speaking to your heart. He can mend your broken heart. He can cleanse the dirty and guilty feelings. He can heal the hurts and erase the ugly memories that have haunted you for years. If you're married, the Lord wants to cleanse you through an act of forgiveness towards the one or ones who molested you as a child. You can ask the Lord to heal the memories and accept His Christ-like purity so that your marriage bed will not be defiled in your mind but will be the place of a pure, clean, beautiful, intimate relationship—a special time of communion between the three of you: your husband, Christ and you. Let's pray:

Dear Heavenly Father, I love You and I need You. Right now, Father, I ask You to forgive me for the hatred I've harbored against my father or other relatives or acquaintances who emotionally and physically hurt me. I'm sorry, Lord, I judged him as a physically and emotionally well person, but now I see and understand that he was not well; he was very sick. Right now, Lord, my heart goes out to him. I forgive him for what he did to me. I pray that You will bless and heal him in every area of his life. I pray that he'll find You as his personal Savior and turn his life completely over to You so this won't ever happen again. I release him into Your care and into Your hands, and I release myself of the bondage I've been living in. As of this very minute, I'm set free. I am free, and I thank You for it, Father, in Jesus' name, Amen.

10

Handle With Care

G od gave us tongues to praise Him. Out of joy King David wrote, *"I will bless the Lord at all times: his praise shall continually be in my mouth"* (Psalm 34:1). Besides giving us our sense of taste, our tongues also give us the ability to express ourselves verbally, to show love and concern and to encourage and build each other up. But if our tongues are not handled with care, they become instruments of destruction!

For the past four years I have had the privilege of speaking at the Lundstrom Family Enrichment Seminars. Nearly every weekend of the year I've stood in a hotel or motel corridor and welcomed guests as they arrived for my session. I've observed the expressions of anxiety and depression on many faces.

As I talk with these people, they hesitantly tell me about experiences that have practically destroyed them emotionally, mentally and spiritually. Often, cruel words scarred them in childhood and followed them through life.

I've been shocked to hear what tired and exasperated parents have actually said to their children. Those words have exploded like grenades and injured the little ones, battering them mentally and emotionally.

You and I as parents may quickly forget what we say to our children, but the children will never forget. When they come to us at a bad time and we attack them verbally, we may never realize how final and condemning our words sound. Let me relate some true stories that have been shared at the seminar sessions. They will give you insight into ways in which classmates, teachers, relatives, employers and employees have hurt others through their carelessness.

A mother in Wisconsin openly objected to the young man her daughter was going to marry. On the wedding day, she told her daughter, "I'd rather have attended your funeral than this wedding!" At the seminar, the young lady revealed, "My husband and I have been married ten years now, and that statement has left a wall of dissension between my parents and us."

A short time ago I was speaking at a Bible college in North Dakota when an unhappy young lady approached me. Starting to cry, she said, "Gloria, from the time I was a little girl, my dad and mom have told me, 'You're ugly! No one will ever want to even look at you!' So all my life I have been a loner, afraid to try to make friends for fear that they would make fun of me. I hate myself because of my looks!"

In a fit of rage, a father in Wisconsin screamed at his teenaged daughter, "You've caused so much trouble! When you were born, we should have put you in a sack and drowned you in the river!" The father could have been half-kidding, but his daughter accepted what he said as what he meant and she still thinks, "My dad hates me! He wishes I were dead!''

In South Dakota a lady said, ''I live in fear that my husband will leave me.'' When I asked her why she elaborated, ''While I was growing up, my parents repeatedly told me, 'You're sloppy!' One day my dad said, 'If you ever get married, your husband will leave you because you are the world's worst housekeeper!''' The lady went on to say, ''Now I work on my house day and night. I'm a slave to it because I can't get rid of the fear that my husband will leave me if the house isn't always in perfect shape!''

One young lady from Kansas related what her mother had snapped at her. ''I was pregnant with you and had to get married. If it weren't for you, I could have finished high school, gone to college and done all the things I had my heart set on. Because of you, I'm nothing!'' The daughter couldn't get over the horror of rejection and unjust guilt for messing up her mother's life.

In Montana, a lawyer stood to his feet and began to cry. ''Gloria, I've always had to compete with my father. He was a fine lawyer, very well respected; everybody loved him. One day when I was in second grade my teacher looked at me sternly and asked, 'Why aren't you like your father? He's respected and is a great man. Do you know what? You will never amount to anything.' Since that day I have struggled all my life to be a somebody—but every time I try to achieve a goal, I hear the words of that teacher ringing in my ears, 'You'll never amount to anything.'''

In the same seminar another tall, muscular-built man stepped forward. I questioned, ''Do you need an inner healing of bitterness against someone?''

Nervously he answered, ''Yes, I have had a bitterness against my father since I was a young lad, 5 or 6 years old. We lived on a farm, and as little kids, we used to put gas in the old tractor and run it around the farm yard. One day my father looked at me and ordered, 'Don't use any more gas out of the tank, we're almost out and I need it.' He thought the gas man was going to come the next day, but he didn't. A few days later when he went to fill the tractor, the tank was empty. He stormed across the farm yard, picked me up and yelled, 'Did you take all the gas out of the tank?'

"'No, Dad, honest I didn't.'

"He accused, 'You're lying.' He dragged me to the barn, took a big leather strap that he used to fasten to the side of the horse, and he beat me until I thought I'd either bleed or die from the pain. He left me there crying. I was crushed; not only because of the pain, but because he didn't believe me.

"The next day we were out in the farm yard when the bulk gas truck pulled in. Out jumped the driver who began to apologize to my father, 'I'm sorry I didn't make it out here a couple of days ago. I was so busy. I hope you didn't run out of gas!'

"Those words echoed as I stood right by my dad. Then he knew I wasn't lying. But he never once came back and said, 'I'm sorry that I strapped you. I'm sorry I accused you of lying.'

"I've never forgotten that incident and I've held a deep bitterness against him for all these years. I need an inner healing of this unforgiveness in my heart towards my father."

In Cedar Rapids, Iowa, a beautiful talented teenager approached me after a teen seminar. "How can I get my mother to love me? When I come home from school she blurts out, 'I hate you, I hate you.' I keep begging her, 'Mother, why do you hate me?' She always answers, 'I've always hated you—and I always will.'"

A stately, well-poised grey-haired woman from Kansas pleaded, "Please pray that I can accept myself as God accepts me. I desperately need an inner healing of words spoken to me as a child. When I was three years old, I was critically burned in a fire, leaving scars all over my face and body. My family couldn't afford plastic surgery, so my scars left me a laughing-stock for everyone to make fun of. One day visitors were coming to our farm and Mom panicked. 'Edith, you're so ugly. Go run and hide under the big oak table, and stay there until our guests leave.' I was so hurt that after that every time somebody came to our house, I immediately hid under the big oak table with the long lace tablecloth and stayed there in fear and embarrassment until they left. I can still hear those words, 'You're ugly, you're so ugly.'"

Another time, a well-educated, well-dressed business woman asked for private counseling. When we stood face to face, I couldn't help but notice that her face was covered with little tumors. "Gloria, I was at your inner healing seminar last weekend." Then her pride broke and she began to expose her hurts. "I need a healing of a memory of what my mother said to me when I was 15 years old. You see, I was born with all these tumors. I've always tried to dress extremely well in order to take people's attention away from my face." Then she rolled up the sleeve on her beautiful blouse. I was shocked at the sight of all the tumors protruding from her fair skin. She continued, "I was born without an opening in my throat. One day in my early teens my mom said to me, 'You've caused us so much grief and trouble, we should have let you die in the delivery room.' Gloria, that really hurt. Then, when I was 15 years old, I was going to a banquet. I bought a new white dress and got my hair fixed at the beauty shop for the first time. I was so proud of how I looked. I ran to my mother and asked, 'How do I look?'—hoping for her approval. My mother said bluntly, 'You're ugly, and more than apt to stay that way.'" This lady began to sob, "All my life I've felt so ugly because of her words, and wished I were dead. Please help me!"

The Bible states matter-of-factly, *"Death and life are in the power of the tongue: and they that love it shall eat the fruit thereof"* (Proverbs 18:21). What a sobering Scripture. What are you giving your child? What are you giving others: death or life?

Take inventory of what you're saying as well as how you are saying it. The Lord has dealt with me on this subject and He's helping me to guard my tongue, my tone of voice, my spirit and my actions.

Not long ago I went to my daughters and asked, "Have I ever said anything to you that has hurt you or left a wall between us?" To my surprise, both LaShawn and LaDawn brought up something that I'd said two years before. I wasn't feeling well at the time and I was very impatient. I raised my voice and by the intonation of my voice they thought I was mad and didn't like them. I immediately asked them to forgive me. I prayed that God would heal those memories—and He did! Now I try to handle every word I say *with care.*

The Tongue With A Torch

Recently we arrived in Sisseton after a strenuous tour. The day was spent unpacking, cleaning the bus, doing the laundry and fighting physical fatigue. By evening Larry and I were physically and emotionally exhausted. The mail was piled high in a large box—unopened. I usually look forward to opening it, but I had a feeling most of it was bills. I decided not to even look at the mail until after I indulged in a good night's sleep. I felt everything would look better in the morning.

Larry and I were still up at 1 a.m. Lee Donovan was so excited to be home he was dragging toys from every corner of his bedroom up to the living room where we were sitting. My eyes kept falling upon that enormous box of mail sitting in the corner of the kitchen. Finally, I announced, "I can't stand it any longer. I have to open up the bills to see how far in debt we are. I'll never sleep knowing all those bills are piled up there." I anxiously—yet reluctantly—ripped open the letters with each bill; they added up to a staggering amount. Finally in desperation I turned to Larry, "Honey, what are we going to do? Where are we going to get the money? With the extensive house repairs it's already peaked $15,000."

Then Larry asked the unpardonable question. (I believe that every woman is entitled to one secret to keep to herself: she should be able to stash away a little money, twenty dollars or so, in a safe place just for herself in case of a rainy day. Larry also knows if all the money's gone, his Norwegian wife has $20 or $40 hidden somewhere to save the day.) I was tired and frustrated about all the bills and emotionally "gone." Then, guess what my husband, Larry, had the nerve to ask, with that mischievious Swedish grin on his face? "Honey, are you sure you don't have some money stashed away somewhere that you can apply to the bills?"

I'm generally a cool, calm and composed person, but

that did it! I threw the letters down, looked at him and exploded, "What do you want? Hey, I've given you everything I have. I've given you my speaking engagement offerings, I've given you my money from books and seminars. I don't have any more. Do you hear me? What do you want? My blood?" Sounds like an irrational woman at 2:00 in the morning, doesn't it?

Little did I realize that Lee Donovan, 4 1/2 years old, was sitting by the stairway listening to every word I said. He came running and crying, "Don't holler at my daddy, he's a good daddy. Why are you hollering at him?"

I'm sure he hadn't heard me raise my voice for over two years. I was shocked to hear myself respond the way I did. Donovan's eyes were big, and worry saturated his usual carefree face. I calmed down and explained, "Donovan, everything is just fine. You just crawl in Mom and Dad's bed and look at the story books."

He added, "You're mad at my daddy and I don't want you to be mad at him."

I assured him, "I love Daddy. I'm just tired; go jump in bed." He did, and the conversation between Larry and me went back to normal. It was all over—so I thought.

At the breakfast table the next morning we were all enjoying French toast, eggs and sausage. After a few moments Larry and the girls excused themselves and left the table. Donovan sat there with his head resting in his hands on the table, deep in thought. Just as I was going to get up and clear the table, he looked up at me and asked, "Mom, why were you mad at my dad last night? Why did you holler at him? He's a good dad."

"Yes," I confirmed, "he's a very good daddy."

"Well, why did you holler at him?"

"Well, honey, Mama was just tired. And, he was asking me some questions and I was telling him the answers...."

He interrupted, "Mom, Dad doesn't have to mind you. He's the boss. He's the head of the home."

I sank deeper into the wooden chair, almost choking with embarrassment.

He looked me right in the eye, and quizzed, "Mom, did you tell him you were sorry for hollering and did you ask him for forgiveness?"

By this time his sermonette had really stabbed deeply in my heart, for I knew I hadn't asked Larry for forgiveness. Then that verse in Ecclesiastes 11:1 seized me, *"Cast thy bread upon the water, for thou shalt find it after many days."* Donovan has heard me share about inner healing and forgiveness many times. That was the bread I had cast upon his life, and now it came back to me. I was so hurt to think I had let him down. I thought, I won't lie to him, but I'll just nod my head; maybe he'll think that means "yes." So I let my head drop a few inches, and he pointed his finger at me and exclaimed, "I don't really think you did. I think you're just putting me on."

That did it! I admitted, "Donovan, you're right, Mama didn't apologize, but I will."

He added, "Mom, do it right now and ask him to forgive you. Then kiss him like you did the night you got married."

That broke the ice. I picked him up and loved him— set him down on the kitchen chair and again called for Larry. He came upstairs and I asked him to sit down at the table.

I apologized, "Larry, I'm sorry I raised my voice

last night. I was wrong. I love you and I want to ask you for forgiveness." Donovan's face was exploding with a big grin. Then his eyes searched Larry's face.

"Gloria, I forgive you. I love you, honey. You were just fatigued and under a lot of pressure. You're forgiven. It's all O.K."

Then I felt a little foot kicking my knee under the table. I looked at Donovan and he whispered, "Don't forget about the kissing part."

So, I quickly walked over to Larry, kissed him on the forehead and told him that Donovan wanted us to forgive each other and kiss like we did on our wedding night. We embraced, kissed, and then Donovan jumped up on the chair, threw his arms around our necks and exclaimed, "Hey, I want some of that, too!"

That was a special lesson on forgiveness for me. Children need to know and feel harmony in the family. Harsh or loud words send fear and insecurity within their hearts even if they aren't able to tell you.

If there is dissension in your family, between you and your mate or you and your children, chances are that it's been caused by careless words. The dissension may even be in your church or your place of employment. I urge you to break down the barrier of your pride, go in openness and honesty to others and ask them if you've ever said any words that have caused bitterness to come between you. If the answer is yes, ask for forgiveness.

Pray the prayer I've prayed to re-dedicate my tongue to Christ:

Lord, take my tongue; anoint it with Your love, understanding, and patience that will glorify and edify my mate, children, relatives and everyone I come in contact with. Thank you, Lord, Amen.

11

The Grave of Guilt

*L*et's talk about guilt. What is it? The Bible dictionary defines guilt as "deserving of punishment
because of a violation of law or conduct."

Webster's dictionary says, "Guilt is the fact of
having done a wrong or committed an offense. A feeling
of self reproach from believing that one has done a
wrong."

Guilt and conscience go hand in hand. Our conscience
tells us the difference between right and wrong. Take,
for example, a car. When something goes wrong with
the engine, a red light flashes on the control panel of
the dash. The same principle applies with us. Every
time we violate a basic principle of right and wrong, a
little "conscience light" glows within us, telling us
something is morally wrong and needs immediate
attention. It's our warning light to let us know we have
stepped out of our God-given boundary lines. Even
though our conscience reminds us when we have done
wrong, *it is not sufficient to make us do right.*

The Bible tells us the condition of our conscience is determined by our conduct. We have a "good conscience" by doing what is in harmony with God's standard. The writer of Hebrews said, *"Pray for us, for we are sure that we have a clear conscience, desiring to act honorably in all things"* (Hebrews 13:8, RSV). It says his good conscience was dependent upon honorable conduct.

When we do wrong we have what the Scripture calls a "defiled conscience." *"...and their conscience being weak is defiled"* (1 Corinthians 8:7). Corrupt conduct "stains" our conscience making us feel guilty. In a nutshell: sin is the culprit that gives us a guilty conscience. Sin can easily be defined as "missing the mark." Paul says, *"For all have sinned and come short of the glory of God"* (Romans 3:23). But through Christ we can be changed from "I have sinned," to "I am saved."

When a man continues in sin, error and corrupt living, he reaches the point where his conscience no longer responds to right or wrong. So don't condemn the "warning signal" within you—praise the Lord for making you aware of what is wrong, and then take care of the problem.

Very few days go by that our conscience doesn't inform us that we've violated God's standards or laws. Unless we are able to deal with those violations, we will gather a load of unresolved guilt which will, in turn, cause many problems and prevent us from being the kind of free people God designed us to be.

Kinds Of Guilt

There are two types of guilt: one is a legitimate guilt that occurs when you willfully do wrong or go against God's laws or ordinances. It may be theft, murder, adultery, neglecting your family, lying, verbally abusing someone, cheating, shirking your responsibilities, obesity, drugs, alcoholism—just to name a few. The guilt that accompanies these sins is a just and legal guilt. The "red warning light" of agony, pain, sickness and bitterness will not dim until the sins that are causing it are forgiven and forsaken. Until you openly admit your guilt to God you will be miserable. Worse yet, you may not be yielding to the call of God to repent and you are becoming more insensive and callous every day. I urge you to call out to God for forgiveness. He will then forgive you and release you from your burden of guilt. When you've done that, your inner warning light of conscience will read, "all clear."

So many people lament, "But I just know God can't love me, I know He can't forgive me. I'm too wicked." That's not true. Jesus came and died on the cross to pay the price for *all* sins for *all* people.

In his thought-provoking book, *The Screwtape Letters*, C. S. Lewis satirizes the daily routine in hell and the headaches of the hard-working demons who just try to put in an "honest" day's work fouling up Christian's lives. One of the most successful tactics the demons used to neutralize their enemies (Christians) was to get them to dwell on all their failures. Once people began feeling guilty about their performances in the Christian life, they were no longer any threat to Satan's program. Satan really does use these tactics because he knows they work!

Here is a testimony of a lady with legitimate guilt... who received legitimate forgiveness:

The young distraught woman came running up to me, grabbing my arm. "You've got to help me, I'm desperate!" I tried to calm her down, but her eyes flashed with fear. Her husband quickly came up beside her and gave me a look that said, "You've got to help us." I put my arms securely around her and the three of us walked to the pool area of the convention center where we could escape the busy crowd.

"Gloria, you spoke about the 'grave of guilt' during your session. I've been thrown into that grave and it's caving in on me." She continued to relate her story, "My husband was already married when I first met him. He was unhappy with his marriage, so we soon started seeing each other. We decided to get married, and he filed for divorce. That was a terrible experience. He had two children and his wife demanded alimony, leaving us with hardly anything to live on. I became very bitter against her because her demands caused problems between my husband and me.

"One night, in a fit of rage, I screamed at my husband, 'The best thing that could ever happen to us would be for your ex-wife to get killed in a car accident—that would solve everything!'

"Oh, Gloria, a few months later we received a phone call telling us the shocking news that my husband's first wife was killed in a tragic car accident. The two children survived. I was shocked, hurt, frightened and guilt-stricken. It's been a mess. Now we have the two children, but every time I look at them, I hear my terrible words over and over again. I know it's my fault their mother is dead, and the children cry for her all the time because they miss her so much. What can I do? I'm wracked with the pangs of guilt!"

I explained to her, "You don't have to let this guilt devour you—even though you thought, expressed and wished death on this young mother. God is here this very moment to forgive you—He won't bring her back to life but He can cleanse and forgive you.'' She cried, ''Please pray with me, I don't even know how to pray.'' After she gained her composure I asked her to pray after me, ''Dear Father in Heaven, I come into Your presence so unworthy of Your love and understanding, but because I love You and I need You so desperately, I come in the name of Jesus. I ask You to forgive me for my terrible thoughts and words. Please forgive me. I'm sorry. Release me from this guilt, Lord. I also ask that You'll give us a supernatural love for these children so we can be godly parents and lead them to Christ. Lord, set me free—in the name of Jesus. I love You, Amen.''

She kept gripping my hands tighter and tighter. I looked into her face and it appeared God opened a flood gate of tears, cleansing this beautiful young lady. Looking up she said, ''Gloria, I feel so clean.'' Then turning to her husband whose face was also tear stained, she announced, ''I'm starting over, we're both starting over—clean before God. Now with God's help, let's love and raise your children—I guess I should say, 'our children.' Let's hurry and go home. I just want to hold and love them.''

Praise God for the freeing power of forgiveness!

Everyone at one time or another has experienced a guilt-trip over something he or she thought, said or did! Then Satan attacks us, using guilt to cause sleepless nights, nightmares, sickness, self-condemnation and all that goes with it. The guilt this young girl experienced came upon her because of hateful words she said in a fit of rage.

An extremely beautiful 23-year-old girl from Superior, Wisconsin, approached me after hearing me speak and asked if we could find a quiet place to talk.

"This guilt is killing me. God doesn't love me; He won't forgive me. I won't go to heaven. There's just no hope for me. I can't stand this guilt any longer." I reassured her that God loved her, but she wept, "No, no, you don't understand what I've done. When I was 19 I was dating the guy I'm now married to. One night we went too far and I got pregnant. We were young, wanted to finish college and had no money. The last thing we needed was a baby in the midst of our problems. Finally, at wit's end, we decided that my having an abortion was the only solution.

"I was two months pregnant when I went to the clinic. I was terrified, filled with mixed emotions. During the abortion I kept thinking, 'I want this baby—no, we can't have this baby!' While I was lying there I guess I kind of "freaked out" because I thought I heard a baby cry. I went to pieces, crying hysterically. Finally someone had to give me an injection to calm me down. When I left I felt so guilty. All I could think of was, 'I killed my baby, I killed my baby!'

"That was four years ago. A year later we got married, but every night since that happened I've had a nightmare. Every time I see a baby I hear that same voice accusing me, 'You killed your baby, you killed your baby.' My husband has wanted a baby so badly ever since we got married three years ago, but I won't agree to because I'm afraid that because of my sin God will punish me with a deformed child. What can I do? I'm a wreck—I'm scared to death!"

I looked into her tense, tear-stained face; she was such a beautiful young girl but just completely crushed. I encouraged her with the fact that the Bible says, *"If we confess our sins, he is faithful and just to forgive us our sins, and to cleanse us from all unrighteousness"*

102

(1 John 1:9). I continued, "You just have to believe God wants to free you, not punish you."

She cried, "But haven't I gone too far?"

"No," I reassured her. "We always have free access to the throne of God for His forgiveness." I invited her to pray. We joined hands and prayed that the strongholds of Satan would be released from her life. We agreed that Christ would completely set her free. We rebuked Satan of any control over her mind, soul and body.

In a few moments we both felt the presence of God move through us. Immediately the most beautiful peace surrounded us, expressing the closeness and presence of God. I felt like someone lovingly wrapped us in a warm blanket. She began to smile and a shine radiated from her. She was completely calm. She put her arms around me and quietly said, "I'm free. Oh, I feel so peaceful, so clean. I feel so pure—my guilt is gone, Gloria, it's really gone!"

Isaiah 43:25 says, *"I, I am He who blots out your transgressions for my own sake, and I will not remember your sins"* (RSV).

Praise the Lord! Not only does He wipe out the guilt after the act of forgiveness, but He *forgets* them!

As a man once said, "God throws our guilts and sins into the deepest sea—and God doesn't go deep sea fishing!" In other words, once He has cast them into the sea of forgetfulness, He doesn't turn around with a fishing pole and drag them back up again; they are eternally G-O-N-E!

The second type of guilt is false guilt. In other words, carrying a guilt for something that happened that has *already* been forgiven. The Bible says in 1 John 1:9, *"If we confess our sins, he is faithful and just, and will forgive our sins and cleanse us from all unrighteousness"* (RSV). We need to *accept* the fact of God's forgiveness. For instance, I have several friends who were driving cars when involved in a tragic accident, killing a friend or a member of the family. The guilt that followed them after the accident, death and funeral nearly devoured them. I've heard them cry, "I just know God wants to punish me for what happened. It was my fault; I deserve it." Maybe you've been involved in an experience similar to the "if only" stories of accidental deaths. You must *will* to accept God's forgiveness.

After a speaking engagement in Garden City, Kansas, a striking 6'5" man stopped me. "Gloria, this guilt is more than I can take. I'm about to lose my mind. You've got to pray for me." He towered a foot over me. I thought to myself, "What on earth could shatter this confident-looking person?" In just a few minutes, I knew.

"I have a sweet wife and I had a daughter two years old. Last summer she was outside playing and ran behind my pickup as I was driving out of the driveway. I felt a bump as I backed up—thinking it was a toy or a trike. I jumped out and found my beautiful little daughter crushed to death under the pickup. I can't forgive myself for what I've done. Every night since her funeral I have had a terrible nightmare. I see her lying in her casket with her little frilly white dress on. I can't take it any longer. I don't even want to go to bed."

I began to share with him that the guilt he felt was a torturing guilt put on him by Satan, and he doesn't have to accept it. *God isn't punishing him, it's himself allowing Satan to destroy his peace.* I summoned the man's wife and two friends to join us as we laid hands on him. Sweetly and quietly the Lord began to minister to him, binding the grave of guilt that was destroying him. About five minutes later he looked down at me and commented, "Do you know what? I feel better. I feel different. I feel free from this bondage of guilt."

Don't punish yourself—God is not punishing you. The manger and the cross remind us that Jesus did not come to condemn us, He came to forgive us. He offered Himself ONCE as a sacrifice to take away the sin of the world. That "once" took care of it all. I want to stress this point: Satan can only make us believe what we allow him to. We cannot fight Satan in our own strength; we need to call on God's army. The enemy knows our weakest spots. If you were the captain of an invading army, you would find the least resistance in your opponent's defenses and go in for the kill. That's exactly what Satan does. He is the archenemy of the saints, and he has a way of wiping Christians out—over and over again.

Let's review what guilt does:

1. Guilt destroys our confidence. It causes us to live in fear. I read a story about Sir Arthur Conan Doyle's celebrated trick. He sent a telegram to 12 prominent Englishmen with the warning, "All is found out—flee!" Within 24 hours all 12 fled the country. Why? They were stripped of their confidence and feared something from the past would be found out. Guilt spreads fear within us.

2. Unresolved guilt can cause great emotional stress and physical problems. Guilt drives some people to drink, overeat or talk too much. These people think that by occupying the mouth they will occupy the mind!

3. Guilt may drive a person to a life of reckless abandonment in a frantic effort to escape the condemning finger of conscience. They keep themselves extra busy until their nerves are shattered—driving them to tranquilizers and ulcers. Unfortunately, many of these people suffer nervous and mental breakdowns.

4. Unresolved guilt will cause upheaval in our spiritual lives, robbing us of our fellowship with God. After Adam and Eve rebelled against God, they tried to hide from His presence. Why? Because they didn't want to be confronted with their failure. Sin deadens the desire for the Word of God and fellowship with other believers. People fear that someone will sense their sin and expose it.

5. Guilt will rob us of our spiritual joy. We may play Halloween and wear a happy mask, but the real desire for joy is supressed into a deep grave—leaving us buried alive.

David experienced this loss of joy when he committed adultery with Bathsheba and murdered her husband. He poured out his heart to God in his great Psalm of confession, *"Restore to me the joy of thy salvation, and uphold me with a willing spirit"* (Psalm 51:12, RSV).

Sin had ripped away his joy, but once David experienced the forgiveness of God, he could rejoice and say, *"Blessed is he whose transgression is forgiven, whose sin is covered"* (Psalm 32:1, RSV).

To close this chapter, let me share a favorite Bible story: I'm always moved by the adventures of the Prodigal Son. He left home with his inheritance, spent it all, lost his friends, and finally ended up feeding pigs.

I'm sure he spent time regretting his sins, reliving in his mind the "good times" at home—the comforts, plenty of good food and clothes—and now he had nothing. How touching it is to picture the tattered prodigal son dragging his feet on the homeward stretch, almost too guilt-laden to go home at all. But to his amazement, when his father saw him stumbling up the dusty path, he ran to meet him, threw his arms around his son and loved and accepted him as if he had never left home. His father brought him in, clothed him and gave him a welcome-home party! The father took him back not as a hired servant, but as a beloved son (see Luke 15).

That thrills me! That's exactly how Christ treats us. He sees us guilt-ridden, hurting, dragging along, spiritually starved. He offers us freedom from guilt through forgiveness with *no* condemnation. While we are still hurting, He puts His arms around us, pulls us close to Him and whispers, "Welcome home; I've missed you!"

12

What's God's Blessing Worth?

Forgiveness

After the Lord had been dealing with my heart about forgiveness, it seemed as if a flood-gate of understanding opened; He showed me all the people I had to forgive and also those I needed to ask for forgiveness. One night in the bus I was tossing and turning until finally it dawned upon me that God was trying to wake me up to talk to me. I stumbled up front, propped myself on the couch and draggily asked, "OK, God, here I am. What do you want me to do—pray? For whom or for what?"

The Lord began to speak, "Gloria, I want you to write a tribute to your father and put it in your hometown paper by June 21."

I was still half asleep. Again the Lord repeated the same words. Finally I said, "Well, why? For what reason?"

"Gloria, when you were 15 years old, your dad said something to you one night that really hurt you and has left a scar in your relationship. I want you to forgive him. Write a tribute telling your father how much you appreciate him. Let him know you haven't been a perfect daughter, but that you love him. This will release forgiveness and patch up the little crack in your relationship with him."

I was so tired, I said, "O.K. Lord, I'll do it another time...."

The Lord said, "NOW!"

I argued, "Why now, Lord? I want to sleep. It's so quiet and the bus is still; I want to sleep!"

The Lord again commanded, "Now! What's My blessing worth in your life?" So, I took my pen and paper, wrote from my heart a loving tribute and sent it to the *Sisseton Courier*. It appeared in the weekly newspaper the week of Father's Day. Then I knew why God had given me that specific date. As soon as I mailed the tribute I felt a release of the feeling I had harbored for all those years. I didn't even know it had really existed until the Lord brought it out of my subconscious. But when it was released I felt a new, fuller, neater love for my dad than I had ever had before. I thought I loved him before, but now I loved him more than ever.

I called him long-distance a few days later. I could feel a new, beautiful relationship between us. I'm so glad I obeyed God's urging.

Pride

The Lord always has a way with dealing with my pride. Some time ago we were driving down the highway late one night, and my children and some other members of the team were all chatting. In the course of the conversation, they mentioned that someone they knew had pulled a "shady" deal at a store; this person had switched price tags in order to get an item cheaper. I turned around and expressed disbelief that a so-called Christian would ever do a thing like that. I said, "Well, that's terrible! They should go back and make that right." Just then the Holy Spirit nudged me and said, "Are you throwing stones? Are you judging? Do you think you're so innocent?" And the Holy Spirit flipped out of my memory an incident that happened when I was about six years old.

The "big" city of Sisseton, South Dakota (population 3,500), had just opened a new business called Eckland's Drive In. They sold ice cream cones, root beer, malts and candy. To a kid that sounded like heaven. Only one problem—I didn't have 5 cents, and Mom was at the neighbor's. I was sitting at the old player-piano and happened to look up. My eyes fell upon my little brother's penny piggy bank. My heart leaped—then I thought, "I'll bet I could shake five pennies out of there and no one would ever know it." So I did. I was filled with fear, hoping nobody would walk in. But I succeeded and ran as fast as I could about 10 blocks and courageously ordered my own 5-cent ice cream cone. Oh, was it good!

The next day—the same thought—the same trick. This happened several days in a row. Believe me, I never told a soul. As the Lord brought all this back to me, He said, "Gloria, you cheated in the same way that other person did when you stole from your brother and didn't make it right. You didn't pay it back."

I argued, "Well, Lord, that was 33 years ago, and besides, I'd pay back my brother Wesley the money but I don't even know how much it was...." Guess what?

110

God flashed big numbers in front of my eyes:"83¢"—then commanded, "You pay him back if you want an added blessing to your life."

I promised God I would do it, but several months slipped by. Last Christmas my brother, Wesley Brooks, a pastor in Sartell, Minnesota, came to visit with his wife and family. The Lord said, "NOW!"

I excused myself, went to the bedroom and taped 83 cents on a piece of stationery along with this note:

Dear Brother Wesley,

Here's the 83 cents I stole from your piggy bank when you were a baby and I was 6 years old. I bought ice cream with it. The Lord's been dealing with my heart. Please forgive me for taking the money. I'm returning it because I want God's blessing on my life.

Your sister,
Gloria

Wesley's two sons stood there as he read it aloud after he saw the note and money. He chuckled and thanked me and I joked, "Say, Wesley, maybe someday I'll be getting a letter from you with more than 83 cents!" Ha!

You Ought To Know God Better!

A few months ago Larry and I were going through such a heavy financial struggle I felt I was going to fall apart at the seams. Then the devil began to bug me, "See, Lowell (Evangelist Lowell Lundstrom, my brother-in-law employer) doesn't care! He doesn't care about your needs. If he cared, he would give you a raise!" This seed-thought began to plant bitterness within me. I thought "He (Lowell) doesn't care. He's concerned about everyone else and their needs, but not ours." The feeling began to root deeper and it caused a

111

strain on my spiritual walk with Christ. Then, during the night while we were on a tour of one-nighters through the Midwest, the Lord began to nudge me. "Gloria, you're bitter. You're bitter against Lowell. I cannot bless you until you release your bitterness." Over and over He kept telling me that. But I argued with God. "You speak to Lowell, Lord. Tell him our needs."

The Lord said, "No, you go to him. You release that bitterness and then explain your financial situation to him. Lowell is so busy he doesn't even know that you're hurting. Be open and honest."

Oh, my pride was hurting me. I had never asked Lowell for money before and I didn't want to start now. But the Lord said, "Release your ought." (Mark 11:25 says, *"And when ye stand praying, forgive, if you have ought* [anything] *against any."*) "Your bitterness is keeping My blessing from you. What's My blessing worth in your life?" He kept bringing up that same haunting question.

The next afternoon I paced back and forth by Lowell's motel room door and finally I forced myself to knock. "Come in," Lowell invited. I flew through the door, sat on the bed across from where he was working on a book and blurted, "Hey! Lowell, the Bible says if you have 'ought' against your brother, go to him. Well, you're my brother and I have 'ought.'"

He sheepishly smiled and inquired, "Well, what's up? What's wrong?"

I reported our financial crisis and said, "I've never asked you for any money in 15 years, but Lowell, I don't know where to turn or what to do."

Lowell politely laid aside all his business and replied, "Well, Gloria, I didn't know you were hurting and that you had all that pressure. Sure, we'll figure out some way we can help you out. Why didn't you come to me before?''

I felt so silly. The Lord was right, Lowell did care—he just didn't know. And the Lord was also right—as soon as I blurted everything out to Lowell I felt a complete release of the feelings I had been suppressing for a month.

Lowell handed me a note that said, ''As of the next month we're going to give you a raise.''

I've learned so many valuable lessons in releasing forgiveness and in listening to God's commands. He is always right—that's why He's God!

13

Forgive to Live

Almost everyone I counsel asks, "Why should I forgive that person? He wronged me." Or, "I want to forgive, but I can't." Everyone is faced with this same feeling: "Should I, or shouldn't I?" The human part of us screams, "He hurt me, he made fun of me, he wronged me. Boy, I'll get even with him!"

But God never allows His children the painful luxury of getting even. In fact, He doesn't even allow us the pleasure of nursing hurt feelings. My mother used to tell me, "Self-pity is one luxury, Gloria, no woman can afford." Romans 12:19 says, *"Dearly beloved, avenge not yourselves, but rather give place unto wrath, for it is written, Vengeance is mine; I will repay, saith the Lord."* Yet inwardly we want to repay the vengeance personally. We say, "I'll make him pay. I'll make him miserable. I hope something bad happens to him. He'll be sorry."

All of these feelings and thoughts express, "I'll get even." "Get even" with him if you insist, but remember: revenging an injury makes you even with him—forgiving sets you above him. Revenge breeds hatred. Hatred causes a man to lose friends, a businessman to lose customers, a doctor to lose patients, a preacher to lose parishioners, and on and on it goes.

Christ has given us His example of forgiveness to follow. Jesus said in Matthew 6:14 and 15, *"For if ye forgive men their trespasses, your heavenly Father will also forgive you: but if ye forgive not men their trespasses* [or failures], *neither will your Father forgive you your trespasses* [or failures]."*

Forgiveness is not a choice—it is a command. The command carries a serious warning for all to heed. If we do not forgive, we will not be forgiven. When Jesus told the story of the man forgiven ten thousand talents who refused to forgive a man who owed him "an hundred pence," He added, *"and his Lord was wroth, and delivered him to the tormentors, till he should pay all that was due unto him"* (Matthew 18:21-35).

That principle can be seen in action in marriages, family relationships and also in churches. Whoever has not forgiven father, mother, brother or sister is handed over to torment. Whatever we judge in another, we are doomed to become or reap in our own lives.

Romans 2:1 says, *"Therefore thou are inexcusable, O man, whosoever thou art that judgest: for wherein thou judgest another, thou condemnest thyself; for thou that judgest doest the same things."*

Matthew 7:1 and 2 says, *"Judge not, that ye be not judged. For with what judgment ye judge, ye shall be judged: and with what measure ye mete, it shall be measured to you again."*

Satan delights in damaging family relationships. Mark 3:25 says, "*...if a house be divided against itself, that house cannot stand.*" In other words, it is doomed. Anytime you let unforgiveness take root in a family because of hurts, harsh words, etc.—that's the day Satan will destroy the home of peace, happiness and unity.

There's not a home in America today that has not felt Satan's attack. But there is a key to rebuilding relationships: whether it is a family, or acquaintances, or whoever is involved, that key is forgiveness.

What does it mean to forgive? The Bible dictionary gives this as one definition:

Forgiveness is the giving up of resentment or claim to requital on account of an offense. The offense may be deprivation of a person's property, rights or honor....Forgiveness is conditioned on repentance and the willingness to make reparation or atonement. (I love this next part.) The effect of forgiveness is the restoration of both parties to the former state of relationship. The ground of forgiveness by God of man's sins is the atoning death of Christ.

George Herbert, 17th century English poet, once wrote, "He that cannot forgive others breaks the bridge over which he himself must pass if he would ever reach heaven, for everyone has a need to be forgiven."

Myron Augsburger, author, stated:

"To forgive is costly. To forgive is to carry one's own wrath on the sin of another. The guilty one is released, the offended one frees him, by bearing his own indignation and resolving it in love. God forgives by carrying His own wrath on the sin we've expressed against Him. He absorbs our guilt and

116

makes us free. Forgiveness goes through sin to freedom.''

The Christ of the cross is our great example. Christ suffered for you as an example that you should follow in His steps (1 Peter 2:21). Man owed a debt he could not repay, so God paid a debt he did not owe. God became man—a God-man—in Jesus Christ to be a substitute for us, to pay the immeasurable price, to satisfy the immeasurable debt of our sins. (Christ took the *burdens* of our sins upon Himself, yet He Himself never sinned.) *''While we were yet helpless, at the right time Christ died for the ungodly''* (Romans 5:6, RSV).

All of this summed up means this: the Christ of the cross is our forgiver and our forgiveness. Jesus Christ substituted Himself for us to pay the cost of forgiving. He gave and forgave *all* sin on the cross. We need to accept His forgiveness personally and pass it on to others.

Why Should We Forgive?

1. We need to forgive to release ourselves of the self-condemnation and guilt we have carried that has robbed us of our freedom to be happy and full of joy. Unforgiveness keeps us bound to the past and past hurts—unable to live in the present or future.

2. We need to forgive to release *others* from the personal judgment we have cast upon them.

3. We need to forgive to release God's blessing in our own life. When we harbor unforgiveness, we block not only God's moving in our life, but upon the one we have held a grudge against.

How Can I Forgive?

As I mentioned before, the human nature of man screams, "I won't forgive." We can't forgive on our own, I can't forgive on my own. We have to *will* to forgive. Forgiveness is an act of the will; you *choose* to forgive. When someone wrongs us, it's hard to want to forgive that person. Only after we choose to forgive by following God's command and have been cleansed within will the "feeling" of *wanting* to forgive surface. That feeling will be expressed as, "I can accept and love that person because God has given me a new understanding."

Maybe you argue, "He's no good, he doesn't deserve forgiveness." Wait a minute—let's look at the value God puts on his life:

1. That person you dislike or hate is a man—a human soul created in the image of God.

2. He is a person—a man for whom Christ died—meant to be a child of God. Before you "write him off," or refuse to forgive, stop and think—*no man* is too low to be an object of God's love. *No man*, no matter how wrong, how evil he is, is excluded from God, except if he excludes himself by his own unrepentance. *No man* can be considered worthless, because God Himself died for him. *No man* is unloveable—if God loves him, then God can love him through me. In essence, forgiveness is loving others.

Ralf Luther once explained it this way, "To love one's enemy does not mean to love the mire in which the pearl lies, but to love the pearl that lies in the mire." We're all pearls in God's sight.

Whom Shall I Forgive?

The questions I'm asked the most are: "How do I know if I need to forgive somebody? Gloria, how do I know if I need to ask somebody for forgiveness? How do I know who it is?" Here's a fool-proof way of knowing:

If you're walking down the street and you see someone approaching, and you quickly duck into a store across the street to avoid coming in closer contact with him, that's one sign. Or, if you avoid contact with certain people at work, church, family get-togethers, that's another sign. Or, a third sign is when the thought or sight of someone causes you to bristle inside. Those are indicators telling you that you need to make a step toward the act of forgiveness. Usually they are those closest to us.

Those feelings or signs, believe it or not, are the Holy Spirit telling you there's something wrong. The next step is yours. Even though the other person may be the one who hurt you, chances are he isn't suffering as much as you are. You're the one who's losing sleep and health over it, as well as happiness. Jesus, when He hung on the cross, prayed as recorded in Luke 23:34, *"Forgive them, for they know not what they do."*

There are probably countless people in your life who have said or done things causing bitterness to take root in your life. More than likely, they have forgotten about it, but you haven't. The ones who have hurt you may have been a teacher, doctor, dentist, classmate, brother, sister, relative, employer, employee, pastor, church member, father, mother, etc. When we recognize the hurts and scars and those who have caused them, that's when we need to invite Jesus Christ into those areas of our unforgiveness.

119

When I finally consented to go through the act of forgiveness, I cried, "God, who do I have to go back to? Tell me." I was scared to find out who the Lord would reveal to me. Then the long line-up began: first, I had to forgive God about my attitude toward death. Next, I had to forgive my husband Larry; then a school-teacher, and on and on. I pleaded, "Oh, God, how can I confront these people face to face?" The Lord said, "Gloria, write them a note, and write these words, 'Thinkin' of you today. Please forgive me for anything I've done to hurt or offend you. I want God's blessing in my life.'" Then He added, "Put it in an envelope, stamp it and take it to the post office and mail it. When you drop it in the mailbox, you are released of your unforgiveness; you are free—free to receive My blessing. You've also released My blessing to begin working in the other person's life."

I'd never thought of it that way before. My unforgiving spirit had actually blocked God from being able to work in another person's life. That terrified me. I cried, "Oh, God, I'm sorry." I began to go back to those people and started writing letters as fast as the Lord showed me those who I had "ought" against. Praise God, it was true. As soon as I wrote the note or spoke the words, "Please forgive me," I felt a surge of God's blessing on my heart, life and ministry. It was and still is exciting. You must choose to forgive.

There are two kinds of offenses that we need to define:

1. *Unknown offense*—This offense occurs when you know someone is deliberately avoiding you or treating you coldly. In this case you may have unknowingly done or said something that left the

wrong impression, offending them, causing hard feelings or bitterness. If you feel this could be the case, write a note and say, "Just a note to let you know I'm concerned about our relationship. Evidently I somehow offended or hurt you somewhere or sometime. Please forgive me and pray for me that I'll be more careful to guard my tongue so as not to hurt others. God bless you. Waiting to hear from you."

2. *Known offense*—After time spent in prayer, God will show and reveal the hurt or offense you've caused someone by your attitude or actions. The Lord will bring back the place, time, event and word or action that caused the gap in your relationship with a person or persons. After God has revealed this to you, write a note expressing, "Thinking of you today. I'm writing this note to ask you for forgiveness for the hurt, embarrassment or bitterness I caused you. I wasn't acting as a child of God when I said those things (or did something). By the grace of God, I want to change and have God's blessing working in my life. Please forgive me and pray for me—I want God's blessing in my life."

David Augsburger, in his book *Caring Enough To Forgive,* explains what is demanded of both the forgiver and the receiver of forgiveness:

This process is equally demanding for the giver and the receiver of forgiveness. Each requires a willingness to both trust and risk. For the forgiver, there must be the willingness to see another's words and actions as genuinely repentant so that suspicion and mind-reading are laid aside, the past is dismissed, and the present transaction is made with integrity. There must be the willingness to trust the other by risking being wronged again, even though the person wrongs you repeatedly, "seven times in the day," Jesus said (Luke 17:4, RSV). That's every hour on the hour. And for those who keep score, multiply it even more (see Matthew 18:22).

There must be willingness to be open to new ways of relating, new experiments in being more real with each other because of the ground gained by the hurt and the healing.

Receiving forgiveness is an equal risk. In accepting forgiveness from another, there must be the willingness to affirm clearly and candidly that my repentance is genuine and that I am choosing to change. There must be a willingness to trust my own responses and to risk being freely spontaneous again even as I know that this could lead to my repeating the failure and re-opening the wound.

There must also be the willingness to be open again with both candor and caring. I will not be inhibited by past failure and timid about contributing to our relationship lest failure follow failure and my repentance be questioned as inadequate and insincere. Forgiveness allows me to risk being myself fully and freely. So I can be close to you without fear, moving back into intimacy without anxiety shooting up and paralyzing my ability to be near you.

These are the steps that lead to our mutual recognition that intentions and new directions are genuine in authentic repenting, and right relationships are now either restored or achieved.

And this is forgiving.

Benefits, Benefits, Benefits

Those are demands, but look at what you receive. You receive mended homes, good health, peace of mind, restored relationships with loved ones, and a renewed relationship with Christ. You have a brand-new exciting life to look forward to—a new explosion like I've had in my life; a life without anger, rejection, guilt and hatred that takes away your joy. You can wake up after a good night's sleep and look forward to an exciting day of feeling Christ and His love dwelling within you.

SCRIPTURES RELATED TO FORGIVENESS

The following verses will remind you of the commands, promises and faithfulness of God. Tear these out and take them with you—using the strength of God's Word to help you in your relationships with other people.

Matthew 5:24 (KJV)—*"Leave there thy gift before the altar, and go thy way; first be reconciled to thy brother, and then come and offer thy gift."*

Matthew 6:14-15 (KJV)—*"For if ye forgive men their trespasses, your heavenly Father will also forgive you: But if ye forgive not men their trespasses, neither will your Father forgive your trespasses."*

Matthew 18:18 (KJV)—*"Verily I say unto you, Whatsoever ye shall bind on earth shall be bound in heaven: and whatsoever ye shall loose on earth shall be loosed in heaven."*

Matthew 18:21-22 (KJV)—*"Then came Peter to him, and said, 'Lord, how oft shall my brother sin against me, and I forgive him? 'til seven times?' Jesus saith unto him, 'I say not unto thee, Until seven times: but, Until seventy times seven.'"*

Mark 11:25-26 (KJV)—*"And when you stand praying, forgive, if ye have ought against any: that your Father also which is in heaven may forgive you your trespasses. But if ye do not forgive, neither will your Father which is in heaven forgive your trespasses."*

2 Corinthians 2:11 (KJV)—*"Lest Satan should get an advantage of us: for we are not ignorant of his devices."*

Ephesians 4:32 (KJV)—*"And be ye kind one to another, tenderhearted, forgiving one another, even as God for Christ's sake hath forgiven you."*

Colossians 3:13 (KJV)—*"Forbearing one another, and forgiving one another, if any man have a quarrel against any: even as Christ forgave you, so also do ye."*

I would like to share with you some quotations I've gathered through the years. Clip these out and put them where you can see them every day.

"Forgiving a person is clearing his record with us, and transferring the responsibility for any punishment to God." (Bill Gothard)

"Forgiveness is a gift we can give to a person—a gift that enriches the life to which it is given, and enriches the life bestowing it."

"Forgiveness opens life to the healing that comes when love and friendship are allowed to flow through the heart."

"Forgiveness deepens relationships and allows them to survive the day-to-day misunderstandings that are so much a part of living."

"Forgiveness is the one ingredient needed to deepen friendships and cement relationships. Without forgiveness there will be brokenness beyond repair."

"Forgiveness is one heart saying to another heart that they treasure the person more than the problem, and desire a friendship at any cost."

"Forgiveness is a two-way street. It requires the open heart of the forgiver, as well as the acceptance of the forgiven."

"Forgiveness, when it replaces resentment and bitterness, works a double-miracle. It touches the forgiver with the atmosphere of love and it touches the forgiven with the atmosphere of acceptance."

"Unforgiveness is like having a dead body chained to you and you keep dragging it around behind you."

David Augsburger has written a tremendous book entitled *Freedom of Forgiveness*. I would like to share these quotes with you:

"Forgiving is the result of complete forgiveness, it is never the means. It is the final step, not the first."

"Forgiveness gives love where the enemy expects hatred. It gives freedom where the enemy deserves bondage. It gives understanding where the enemy anticipates revenge."

"If you hold back forgiveness until the offender deserves it, forget it, that's not forgiveness. Forgive immediately. Forgive when the first hurt is felt. Forgive before the sting is begun to swell."

"The grease of forgiving can reduce the friction and salve the irritation."

"Forgetful forgiveness is not a case of Holy Amnesia which erases the past. No, instead it is the experience of healing which draws the poison from the wound."

"Forgiveness brings new life to our withered hearts, new energy to our paralyzed emotions, new understanding to our frozen feelings."

"The man who receives the forgiveness of God is forgiving of others."

"An unforgiveable heart is unforgiveable."

"Forgiveness is a gift we can give to a person—a gift that enriches the life to which it is given, and enriches the life bestowing it."

14

The Walking Wounded

I hope this book has been an encouragement to you. You could be one of the walking wounded I've written about. You've been deeply scarred and hurt by cutting remarks, haunting memories or deep wounds of rejection. And now you are saying, "Okay, here I am. I'm wounded, but what can I do?"

Allow me to share one last personal experience with you to bring into focus a very important principle.

One bitterly cold fall day when I was six years old, I decided to dig potatoes out of the partially frozen garden plot even though I was instructed, "Do not go out there."

With persistance, along with my own strong will, I was determined to get that potato fork into the hard ground and dig up the last of the potato patch if it was the last thing I did. After moments of struggling with the potato fork, I decided to give it the hardest shove I could muster up. A split second later my foot slipped and the fork buried one blade into my right foot just behind my large and second toes.

I was rushed to the hospital for medical attention requiring several stitches. Then my foot was bandaged. Within a couple of hours it was swollen twice its size and the pain was unbearable. But I liked the bandage—it looked very impressive. The doctor ordered me to come back every two days to have my wound cleansed and re-bandaged and said hopefully in a month the bandage could come off.

When the month was up I rebelled against taking the bandage off because I felt safe and secure with it on. Against my will they took me back to Dr. Peabody. I begged him, "Please leave it on."

He replied, "Honey, we have to take the bandage off and let air get to it so it can begin new skin growth. It will heal more quickly."

I fussed and begged. Finally the doctor conceded to leave it on a few more days.

A few days later, my foot began to feel hot—pain and discomfort set in. But I didn't dare tell my parents. Two days later I finally told my mom about my foot and they took me back to Dr. Peabody. He removed the bandage. His eyes filled with concern as he studied my wound that was now infected and festering. He said, "I knew we should have taken that bandage off. There's only a healthy amount of time a wound should be covered; then it must get air to let it heal and promote new skin growth."

He cleansed the wound, gave me an antibiotic and ordered, "Leave that bandage off but keep the wound clean!" Then he sent me home.

I was scared, but to my complete amazement, in the next couple of days I saw a miracle begin to happen in front of my very own eyes. The festering stopped, the pain and redness disappeared and new pink skin began to heal over what was a deep gash in my foot. In a matter of days the soreness left and I could put a shoe on again and run and play like I did six weeks earlier.

While writing this manuscript, the Lord impressed this experience on my heart and said, "Gloria, tell them to take the bandage off their wounds. Let Me breathe the power of inner healing into their lives. Let Me cleanse the wound."

Friend, there was never a person more deeply wounded by cutting remarks, accusations or rejection any more than Jesus Christ Himself. There He hung on the cross, nails driven through His hands and feet, suspended between heaven and earth between two thieves, abandoned to die. He looked down at the angry mob of accusers and scoffers and then looked beyond their hostility and loved them. He cried to His heavenly Father in the greatest act of unselfish love ever known, *"Father, forgive them; for they know not what they do"* (Luke 23:34). At that moment He removed the bandage of self-pity and hurt, forgave them and gave His life for a lost world that includes you and me. But that wasn't the end.

He was buried, but praise God, three days later He arose from the grave liberated—free from the wounds and hurt that could have kept Him in the grave. He arose triumphantly to live again. What a beautiful example. *"I live; yet not I, but Christ liveth within me"* (Galatians 2:20).

This brings us to one of the most important decisions you may ever have to make. What is God's blessing worth to you? God wants you to remove the bandage and let Him begin healing your hurts. God's healing comes through forgiving. Can you think of a better time than right now to choose to forgive? You can begin to really live! Let me pray with you:

Lord, first I want to praise You for being the greatest example of a forgiver. Because of Your act of forgiveness on the cross, I too, can be free and forgiven. Right now, Lord, I choose to forgive those who hurt and offended me. I go back to my childhood and I choose to forgive my parents, grandparents, brothers, sisters, husband, wife, teacher, pastor, friends, classmates, doctors, policemen, employer, employees, church members, in-laws— every person that has ever caused me to have inner anxiety, scars, bitterness or revenge. Lord, I forgive them all, and I pray that You will bless them. Lord, I ask You to forgive my sins, and I choose to forgive myself for the sins I've committed. I've been hard on myself but now I ask You to cast all my sins into the deepest sea to be forgotten forever. Lord, I believe Your Word in John 8:36, "So if the Son sets you free, you will indeed be free" (TLB). *Thank you, Jesus, I love You, Amen.*

Larry and Gloria Lundstrom have traveled with the Lowell Lundstrom Ministries from Sisseton, South Dakota, for more than twenty years. Larry was director of counseling, photographer for MESSAGE magazine and musician.

Because of the tremendous growth in Larry's family ministry, he and his wife Gloria and three children are now traveling as associate evangelists for the Lowell Lundstrom Ministries.

Larry, an ordained minister, shares in song and a dynamic, Christ-centered message. His evangelistic thrust spans from salvation ministry, encouragement to struggling Christians, how to be spiritually motivated and how to build a strong Christian family.

Gloria sings and complements this ministry with teaching sessions. She has an Inner Healing Seminar which has proven immensely successful.

Larry and Gloria's family includes their children LaShawn, keyboard artist and singer; LaDawn, drummer and singer; and their son Lee Donovan. Traveling with the family are musicians and other team members.

The Larry Lundstrom Family is available to minister in the following areas:

1) Sunday Morning Worship Service

2) Evening Rallies

3) Inner Healing Seminar by Gloria

4) Motivational Seminars and Luncheons

For information on scheduling the Larry Lundstrom Family in your area, phone (605) 698-3939 or write Larry Lundstrom Family Ministries, Box 99, Sisseton, South Dakota 57262.

Larry Lundstrom Family

MINISTRY MATERIALS

FREE AT LAST!
by Gloria Lundstrom
Gloria Lundstrom, wife of Larry Lundstrom, shares how to be set free through forgiveness. God has given her a special ability to help people be released from harmful and hurtful emotions collected over the years. You can experience the peace and excitement of personal freedom by reading and responding to this great book of ministry.

MB-72 $4.00

A RENDEZVOUS WITH VICTORY
by Gloria Lundstrom
What do you do when you have been diagnosed as having cancer? This interesting 48-page booklet reveals the personal struggles involved when the doctors at the University of Minnesota Hospital gave Larry Lundstrom their verdict. You will find strength and encouragement from this real-life experience.

MB-45 $.75

FREE AND FORGIVEN
by Gloria Lundstrom
This 3-cassette tape series will be a tremendous blessing to you. You will be able to experience great personal freedom by listening to these life-changing messages. Here is the best of over 5 years of Gloria's seminar speaking: Free To Be Me (How to be Set Free Through Forgiveness); Self-Acceptance: Key to Survival and Soaring Above Your Struggles. These tapes will help you enjoy a liberated Christian life. Beautiful sturdy vinyl binder included.

MC-75 $15.00

JUST FOR KIDS

Features album, cassette (music and sound track) and lyrics.

Praising the Lord • The Fastest Song • Little David • Jesus Loves Me • It's A Happy Day • The B-I-B-L-E • Pound, Pound, Pound • Grandma and Grandpa • Butterfly • Suzy's Prayer • I'm Not Afraid of the Dark • That's Why I Love the Lord • He's Watching Over Me • I'm His Friend Each Day • God Sent an Angel

MR-35 $12.00

JUST FOR KIDS SONGBOOK

A beautifully illustrated songbook containing words and music to all the songs from the ''Just For Kids'' record album. A great gift to help little singers and musicians get excited about music and improve their singing and listening skills.

MB-67 $3.95

THE LARRY LUNDSTROM FAMILY COLLECTION

NEW

I'm on My Way to Heaven • When I Prayed Through • Praise the Lord • I Sing Jesus • The B-I-B-L-E • Come Spring • It's Great to Be a Christian • Bigger Than Any Mountain • Tears Are a Language • I'll See You in the Rapture • That's Why I Love the Lord • A Happy Way to Live • Now You Know • This Old House

MR-64 $8.00

HEAVEN'S ANSWER FOR THE HOME
Enrich your marriage! Make your home a happier place. Learn to prepare your children for the days ahead. Find personal fulfillment through life's most intimate relationship. These topics and more are discussed in this helpful volume.

TB-39 $3.50

LOWELL
What compels a man to spend over 300 nights a year for 25 years traveling across the country singing and preaching the Gospel? Here, in the words of his family and friends, is unique insight into a special man and his ministry.

MB-34 $3.50

GOD'S GREATEST PROMISES
Over 330 pages of God's promises printed topically—a must for everyone. Here is a quick and easy guide to the promises of God (KJV). This special edition is bound by a beautiful genuine bonded leather cover. A great devotional aid—an excellent gift.

MB-50 $19.95

OUR FAVORITE RECIPES

Here are over 400 delicious recipes collected from friends all over the United States and Canada who have shared their favorite dishes with the Lundstroms during their past 25 years on the road. Arranged in easy-to-follow categories, this cookbook—with photos, inspirational thoughts and scripture verses—will be an exciting addition to every kitchen. Unique spiritual helps section included.

MB-17 $9.95

WHAT'S COMING NEXT?

An encouraging look into the exciting future God has planned for you! If you have avoided Bible prophecy because you thought it was too difficult, too speculative, or simply because it didn't inspire you, then you will enjoy reading this captivating book. Lowell Lundstrom shares easy-to-understand biblical prophecies along with exciting spiritual truths. 360-page large "speed-read" type.

MB-49 $4.95

NEW

IF YOU'RE OVER THE HILL YOU OUGHTA' BE GOIN' FASTER
by Carl Malz

Carl Malz, associate evangelist of Lowell Lundstrom, explains how to get the best out of the rest of your life! This delightful book will help you laugh at the past and give you courage to face your future. Chapter titles include: Gray Is Great!; Feeling Better God's Way; The Antidote for Loneliness and Counterattack. This book is a great resource for friends or loved ones who are retiring or looking forward to it.

MB-70 $3.50

LARRY LUNDSTROM FAMILY
ORDER FORM

QTY.	ITEM NO.	DESCRIPTION	PRICE EACH	TOTAL PRICE

Method of Payment

☐ Money Order   ☐ Master Card   ☐ Visa   ☐ Check

Credit card No. ☐☐☐☐☐☐☐☐☐☐☐☐☐☐☐☐

Expiration date ☐☐☐☐☐

Telephone No. ( ) _____

Signature _____

TOTAL AMT.
ENCLOSED
(in U.S. dollars)

NAME _____

ADDRESS _____

CITY _____ STATE _____ ZIP _____

Send order to:

LUNDSTROM MINISTRIES
Sisseton, South Dakota 57262